GUERRILLA CO

Glen McCoy

First published in 2011 by Management Books 2000 Ltd
Forge House, Limes Road
Kemble, Cirencester
Gloucestershire, GL7 6AD, UK
Tel: 0044 (0) 1285 771441
Fax: 0044 (0) 1285 771055
Email: info@mb2000.com
Web: www.mb2000.com

British Library Cataloguing in Publication Data is available

ISBN 9781852526702

THE GUERRILLA WHEEL™
SPEED
1
INTERVENTIONS
2
MASTER PLAN
3
IMPLEMENTATION
4
LOCATION
5
EXPERIENTIAL
6
SENSORY
7
THE
7
TUMBLERS
SIMILES

CONTENTS

To the most gifted coach that any child could ever wish for. The teacher who opened my mind to a world of endless possibilities... I am forever grateful.

Jean Orwin
Lyon Park Junior School, Alperton, Middlesex

ACKNOWLEDGEMENTS

I would like to also acknowledge the following people who have helped or influenced me to make this book possible:

Katrina Wood
Morel Fourman
Myles Downey
V M Ramsay
Steve McDermott
Jonathan Streeton
Mel Wombwell
Derek Houston
Matt Snaith
David Greenberg
Graham Alexander

FOREWORD

by Myles Downey

There are two significant shifts on the horizon that may well result in a far greater need for coaching.

The first of these is happening in a small but increasing number of business organisations that are moving away from traditional hierarchical structures towards something more flexible. Typically many of the key players in the business work from home and use technology rather than travel to a central office.

These new business models don't obey the established rules. On a larger scale I'm thinking of Apple, Google, Wikipedia, Nintendo, Lego and Threadless. Have you heard of Threadless? The clothing company where anyone can send in a design, customers then vote on the designs and those items with the most votes get produced and sold while the winning designers get paid. No decision-making, no focus groups. Threadless is showing market-leading margins and growing fast. A guerrilla approach? Maybe.

The second shift is happening in the thousands of people who go to work every day, particularly the under 30s. They've seen how the generation that preceded them sold their minds and bodies to their companies and were let down. They have a stronger sense of their own autonomy and independence and a desire to preserve both. Interestingly they are also seeking a greater sense of purpose and meaning from their working lives.

These two shifts are surely inter-related, not least because the search for meaningful work, coupled with environmental and economic pressures, is causing the leadership of many businesses to take a stronger ethical stance; to produce goods and services that are of greater quality, last longer and do not deplete the Earth of limited resources. The shifts require people in work to *behave differently*, to have different kinds of relationships both internally in the organization and externally between the organisation's customers and clients.

These relationships are built on principles of abundance, common interest and are also based on trust. That in turn requires different kinds of conversations where self-awareness is key. (Why do we call that emotional intelligence nowadays?).

Engagement then is the name of the game and listening to understand as opposed to gaining a position, is the starting point. Internally that begins to look a bit like coaching. Externally it looks like better customer service.

Coaching is one such different conversation that, in its purest form, is about helping people to discover their own autonomy, their own authority, and their own voice.

I sometimes talk about enabling genius. Genius refers to the vast reserves of potential that reside in each and every one of us and, if you take it back to its Latin root *gignere, genitum; to beget, to produce or cause to happen*, you will see that genius is not genius unless there is a result.

Add to all of this the ever-increasing need in our business organisations to get more from less. So high performance in the workplace coupled with employee engagement is key to the success in twenty-first century organisations, and undoubtedly coaching is *fundamental* in all of this.

It's my view that all of the above will increase the demand for coaching, both externally – provided by executive coaching – and internally provided by coaching from managers to employees. In this context Glen's book *Guerrilla Coaching* is a most valuable addition to the 'coaching cannon'. It stands out for the depth of thought that Glen brings, unhampered by the emerging orthodoxy that focuses so much on ethics and standards without robustly examining what actually works. It stands out because it supports the case that coaching is about delivering results as much as it is about learning and development. And it stands out because it gives access to tools and techniques that are effective and easy to use.

I am confident this book will help a whole new wave of coaching professionals to re-examine their coaching paradigms and consequently become more creative and inspired to help others get greater results from their own undiscovered potential.

Myles Downey,
Author of Effective Coaching
and founder of The School of Coaching

INTRODUCTION

The less effort, the faster and more powerful you will be.
Bruce Lee

The term 'guerrilla' often conjures up images of warfare yet this word when applied to a style of coaching is light years away from aggression bullying or coercion. There's nothing about it that's intended to be negative, overly demanding or demeaning.

Quite the opposite in fact. Well executed, it can be hugely inspirational, extremely insightful, highly results-focused and offers the genuine opportunity of getting greater outcomes *much faster* with less effort. So welcome to the world of *Guerrilla Coaching®*. Though you still may be thinking: What is it exactly?

For now, may I offer you: *a results achievement system based on 7 performance strategies*, which still tells you very little I know, but the complete story is about to unfold.

As far as I'm aware, coaching first originated in the world of sports in the United States under its full title *co-achievement*. Then it was very much about achieving tangible results. However over the years there seems to have been a shift where learning and development occupies greater importance in the minds of coaches particularly managers in companies.

Guerrilla Coaching on the other hand has a much narrower focus. It's been put together to help coaches whatever their role or background to realize and utilise the original secrets of a concept that was responsible for lifting, improving and dramatically enhancing the skills and abilities of people with one major objective: *winning*.

Coaching today is potentially in danger of being misconstrued and lost in time which would be such a loss for individuals and businesses that are *eager to fly*.

Part of my drive to get this book written comes from previous frustrations as a coach, based on experiences over the years where I had failed to help my client because I over looked the basics.

I had temporarily forgotten what real coaching was about in favour of tick-box paperwork and administrative red tape that I was unwisely involving myself with through peer pressure and a lack of courage in my convictions.

Twenty-five years later, I no longer care what people think of my style of coaching. It may not be perfect, but by going back to the fundamentals laid down by the originators of early co-achievement to whom we owe a great deal, I have helped countless people achieve greatness through outstanding results and quite simply I would like to share this knowledge with you.

If you are expecting complex formulae or rocket science then you will be disappointed, yet I still believe that if you are looking for a sharper edge and more power to your elbow as a coach, there will definitely be something in this book for you.

If I can help re-align coaching to its grass roots and re-emphasis the immense power this robust support system can contribute to future human endeavour and achievement, then my task will have been thoroughly worthwhile.

I hope too that I can help kick-start the careers of those who are new to the profession, as well as those seeking a different set of perspectives and tools.

Coaching in Challenging Times

If you live in a big city, scores of businesses around you, probably within a five-mile radius, are wondering how to cope with their future whilst others may be shutting their doors forever. In that same vicinity there are graduates who are desperate to get their first foothold on a career ladder and finding it tough to make an early breakthrough. Even more people are doing a job that was the exactly the same last year, and probably will be precisely the same this; working for the same revenue, not enjoying the journey, yet making no visible attempt to alter their situation, improve their circumstances, or enhance their overall well-being.

A little further a field there will be the inventors and creators of new ideas, products and services. Many are wondering why it's so difficult to get their ingenuity into the marketplace despite working so hard to make it happen. There are the dreamers, who have a specific goal or ambition that they've had for years and are no further forward in making these dreams a tangible reality. There are even successful business people who are so wrapped up with the profitable way things are going, that they are totally oblivious to the many infinitely larger opportunities hovering silently past them overhead.

This then is the exciting world of endless possibilities for coaches the world over. Creating the fabric and infrastructure of Guerrilla Coaching has been my passion for the past ten years and my desire is to add value to what undoubtedly is the fastest growing profession in the world. The only requirements needed from you to explore it further are an open mind as well as some healthy curiosity.

I originally started my student life wanting to become a teacher, but after a very short time I left my degree course utterly disillusioned. My first concern was that many teachers had that questionable life-cycle of school, university and back to school again. Were they simply passing on to a new generation what they'd been given by an older one? I hungered for real-life experiences.

There were also some stark inconsistencies in education that I was uncomfortable with. A primary skill that most teachers are well aware of in learning is that of being able to remember things. If you believe you have a hopeless memory then the chances are probably have. I was very fortunate when I was at school in coming across a memory system that I was able to quickly learn over a couple of days. It helped immensely when revising for exams, and I am in no doubt that in some subjects it made the difference between failing and passing.

I was later to discover that this system was first invented in the 18th Century and is often referred to as the *Memory Peg System*. It's available to anyone who wants to improve their memory and is easy to use. Yet how many school children or students are aware of its existence? As a student teacher I was keen to help my classes have the most fundamental tools at their disposal in order that they become the potential geniuses that I believed they all were. However when I attempted to discuss the inclusion of *memory studies* as part of my teaching classes, I was told that it was not something that made up the syllabus and therefore would be unhelpful and should be omitted.

These early experiences of challenging traditional thinking were I believe, the first sparks of guerrilla coaching firing off within me. A desire to explore the possibility of identifying unorthodox performance strategies that clearly worked and exploring attainment tools that existed yet were usually ignored or overlooked through unhelpful paradigms and sheer ignorance. The challenge wasn't the discovery or use of such tools, it was the resistance from the very people who said they wanted better results yet refused to stray off the beaten path.

Some original 'coach-miners'

Back in 1986, I remember rubbing shoulders with some extremely talented coaches who went off to achieve their own brand of personal success in the years to come.

These coaching super stars included Graham Alexander, Ginny Ditzler, Ben Cannon and Alan Fine. Theses were exciting times and in the '80s money and success was definitely at the top of most people's agenda. With inspiration from books like *The Inner Game of Tennis* by Timothy Gallwey, I found myself unraveling a brand new way of performance 'technology' that few had ever heard of before.

I first stumbled upon the word 'coaching' in the modern day context during a conversation with one of the UK's most respected coaches Graham Alexander, the innovator of the GROW model. He was undoubtedly the inspiration behind my growing interest at the time to make something of this 'new fangled' notion that I was calling consultancy and he was proudly referring to as *coaching*.

Indeed he was using tools in businesses that up to now had only been applied to the sports world. And to my surprise I had already unwittingly started doing it with individuals and entrepreneurs through a business success workshop I'd created called *Denarii*.

Graham had agreed to support me at the initial presentations and soon I realised I was learning new performance secrets from a master. A natural coach, Graham captivated audiences and stimulated a real sense of endless possibility for anyone who truly desired something that they were utterly passionate about achieving. He also introduced me to one of his colleagues Myles Downey and it was an absolute revelation to start my first 'coach the coach' session not in a meeting room, but on a tennis court. More about this presently.

With this great start to my new profession I was to find myself at a crossroads ten years later. I could choose to use the methods of the growing majority in this new fast growing industry, or select a completely different path where no map yet existed. Maybe I'm a rebel at heart, but I opted for the latter.

As the years went by, I became only too painfully aware that my approach would often fly in the face of the coaching traditionalists, some of whom mocked what they saw as a raw maverick style. Yet the evidence from the clients that had engaged me was saying something quite different. I was helping businesses and individuals get desired results in short time frames and since these same clients kept coming back for more I reasoned that I must be doing something right.

'Guerrilla' expanded

The word 'guerrilla' originates from an irregular or unorthodox form of combat where a small group of people took on a much larger force in a 'David and Goliath' situation.

The original guerrilla warfarers would use tactics like ambushes and spontaneous raids against a less mobile and less nimble traditional army.

'Guerrilla' may also be translated as 'little war' in Spanish and has been around since the 1700s. 'Guerrilla' also encompasses the element of surprise and is an extreme form of flexibility in order to strike at a vulnerable point, target or goal within the less agile enemy camp.

Guerrilla combat was also about the attainment of freedom with a clear single focus. These two elements are pivotal in guerrilla coaching where the coach is helping free the thinking of the coachee in a form of mental combat as well as to escape from the self-imposed prison that their old paradigms had created.

In using the word *guerrilla* I also think of engagement, strategy, tactics and the ability to strike while the iron's hot with speed. Finally, having the mobility, both in mind and body, against a seemingly larger opponent creating barriers to one's success. The original guerrilla way of doing things hinged on how to weaken the enemy's strength, forcing them to withdraw or give up quickly. In coaching, the identified enemy often lives in the mind of the coachee. Typically it's the mental chatter that's sabotaging goals and decimating dreams; in effect denying the coachee the success he or she almost certainly deserves. It was also acknowledged that guerrilla warfare was difficult to beat. In my humble opinion, when you use Guerrilla Coaching with an individual, team or group, the methodology and tools though sometimes unorthodox, are designed to create a success platform that dramatically increases the chance of winning as I hope you'll discover.

The Guerrilla Marketing Connection

My interest for creating the guerrilla approach was certainly influenced by the fascinating concept of *Guerrilla Marketing* originally defined by Jay Conrad Levinson in his great book of the same name.

When I saw what Levinson did in marketing using the idea of 'guerrillaship' to help the smaller guy become the bigger guy much more quickly, I could immediately translate his style and approach for my own industry.

What also inspired me in Levinson's book was the idea of using time, energy and imagination rather than financial resources to spearhead success in a corporate environment. He postulated that the primary statistic to measure a business is not sales revenue but bottom-line profitability. With the advent of social media marketing and search engine optimisation, his original thinking was nothing less than visionary. The importance of creating new relationships regularly each month also fits so well with the way business is now being done on the Net today.

So what's the best to use this book?

I thought long and hard about how best to present the information in this book. Given the hundreds of books that have been already written about coaching, the last thing that would be useful to other coaches would be some sort of re-hash of existing books or an intellectual ramble where I end up losing the reader and myself up some theoretical blind alley.

So my chosen approach for my humble literary offering is *notebook style* with diagrams where ever possible to make this a fast, though I hope, informative read.

I cannot take credit for too many of the concepts as I will have learned the fundamentals from other coaches, particularly early on in my career as I felt my way sometimes wearing a blindfold almost; and I hereby formally thank all those who helped inform and educate me.

One other thing on my chosen style for this book is that I tend not to differentiate between tools to use with clients say, and those I am suggesting you may benefit by as a coach. That's because I can't help being a coach myself I suppose and it's in no way inferring that you don't already know the idea or understand the simple point I may be presenting to you. Someone once said to me in a workshop that they already knew 5 of the 7 ideas I offered around *personal effectiveness* in a presentation to a group of business people. What stumped them is when I asked whether that meant they had tried and/or were already using all the five ideas. Their silence confirmed my suspicions. If you come across an idea that you've yet to trial or use for the first time, then may I suggest it's still a *brand new idea*.

What's immensely important for me is that you can dip in and out of the chapters as well as get to grips with the tools I so want to share with you.

Broadly speaking, there are 6 Interventions that refer to areas for coaching, namely: *mindset, strategy, performance, self-discovery, creativity and set skills*. Then there are the 7 Guerrilla Levers. I use the term lever like perhaps a crowbar. This is something you may want to use to get a fast result or immediate outcome while the other coaching tools – and there many of these, are just that... tools to deploy depending on circumstances, desired goals, the type of personality you are dealing with and so on.

Before we get truly started, I would like to take this opportunity of paying homage to all my fellow coaches in the UK as well as around the world.

It always impresses me how serious and passionate most of us are in a profession geared to helping our fellow humans attain not just good results but extraordinary ones. How many other professions instinctively target top performance and push for extraordinary results from the outset?

I also invite you to e-mail me any thoughts, ideas or comments to glen@glenmccoy.com and I promise to answer all correspondence personally.

Finally, I put it to you that there's never been a better time in history *to be a coach*.

Glen McCoy

1

COACHING LEGENDS

So why Guerrilla Coaching and what makes it different to traditional coaching? The number one frustration for any coach, is surely a client failing to achieve the goal they set in consultation with you their coach. When this has happened in the past, two things immediately seem to follow. The first is that I beat myself up inside, possibly also trying to pin some 'blame' on my client so that it doesn't appear that I am totally inept. The second is that I almost certainly lose the client. Either way it's not a great advert for who I am and what I'm offering and there was a point around a decade ago when I had to give the whole matter a great deal of thought in terms of moving forward, or simply giving up coaching altogether.

Fortunately I decided to look at some of the beliefs around coaching that were springing up all over the place as the industry started to grow and develop all over the world.

And whatever brand of coaching you favour as coach, I'd like to suggest some potential misunderstandings around coaching that I needed to address which were instrumental in helping me to shape the guerrilla coaching concept.

There are nine 'coaching legends' that I soon became accutely aware of, and they appear to be as true today as they were three decades ago.

First Legend: Coaching is a Formal Process

In businesses particularly, coaching is nearly always seen as a formal process. When I'm called in to consult with well-known companies it's common place to observe the typical coaching set-up where coach and coachee sit around a table for a one to two-hour session (this can be as long as four hours), invariably using a standard coaching model and drawing from a list of ready-made questions. The reason I get invited, is to evaluate how coaching is being conducted and offer suggestions for improvement. My immediate focus always goes on whether results are being generated rather than initially looking at the coaching model being used.

I'm not aware that the philosopher Confucius ever made any inspirational comments around coaching, however if he had, I'm sure it would be something along the lines of "When coaching doesn't achieve desired outcome, look at person's mindset first, not process and change thinking if needed."

No process or model will ever be effective if the coach and/or coachee are in the wrong psychological place. It's like trying to build a magnificent outdoor eatery that is bang next door to a cement works.

So one of my early discoveries about achieving results with clients was to be more spontaneous and less regimented. I realised that coaching should be a journey of mutual discovery where principally the coachee benefits, but the coach may also learn something as an additional win. When I'm bringing someone into the profession, I certainly do suggest using a framework to coach with otherwise it's very unfair to expect a new coach to deliver the goods with just their wits. However I also endeavour to suggest that they be as intuitive as possible rather than wholly logical and template driven.

Whenever asked whether the less formal guerrilla approach is only for the seasoned professional or whether a new coach could use it, I always enthusiastically encourage anyone to try it provided they have an open mind and their main focus is about tangible results first.

Second Legend: Coaching has to be largely Non-Directive

When I was eighteen I decided to apply to become a Samaritan. I was on a university degree course and thought I'd make use of the hours of free time that I had available in my first year. At the interview I was asked a number of questions but there was a point at which I realised this voluntary undertaking wasn't going to work for me. It was explained how I would work shifts and take calls from members of the public who were depressed or even contemplating suicide. Though I initially got very excited about the chance to help save people from themselves and thought I would be up for the challenge, the interviewer said something that concerned me deeply. She explained that at no time could I offer any advice or a personal opinion to the caller. So I queried what I should say if someone said they were about to make the ultimate decision to do away with themselves.

It was told that I should ask the person to explain their thinking a bit more and then get them to reassess things. Feeling this was all a bit woolly, I asked whether I could simply advise the person that suicide was not an option. She responded with a patronising smile saying that it was not my role as Samaritan to tell people what to do or not to do. Despite being offered the position as a trainee I declined knowing that this non-directive way would not sit comfortably with me because there was too much grey and not enough black and white thinking when it mattered most, and I feel the same about coaching.

It's useful to remember that the word 'coach' originates from the word 'co-achiever'. In the first half of the 20th Century, co-achievers were sports professionals in American football, basketball and baseball who retired at a certain age and then came back to the game and worked with new players who were joining the sport for the first time. Each new guy would then have an experienced co-achiever who'd work with him for the medals, glory and success on a fifty-fifty basis. Even today good sports coaching is based on similar principles. The co-achievement process is about signing up to an equal share of responsibility as well as the results that follow, and this is a fundamental difference between Guerrilla Coaching and traditional coaching. Canadian sports coach Wayne Elderton broadly defines sports coaching in two categories; directive and co-operative. The latter is probably more akin to the guerrilla approach though the directive style has some advantages too. It means that coachees tend to respond quicker if something is not working so the coach can fast-track them to where they should be in a minimal time frame. The advantages of the co-operative approach means that coachees are much more involved in what is a partnership that increases mutual motivation and consequently improves the chances for overall success. Like anything, there may also be a downside. Coachees could ultimately fight against a strong directive approach and the co-operative way does rely more on the coachee's own expertise and background.

Coaches I know who follow the largely non-directive approach always remind me that none of us know everything, and if as coaches we had to have specialist knowledge about every area we were going to work in we'd soon come unstuck and be unable to help the majority of clients. Yet I would suggest that having a more directive and/or co-operative approach is less about specialist knowledge and more about introducing personal responsibility. This is a principle that inspires and ensures maximum commitment in any serious coaching relationship. Specialist knowledge is always helpful and I make a point of doing my research before ultimately coaching a new client. I also feel obliged in broadening my own horizons whilst helping the client to broaden theirs. Also most clients already have all the specialist knowledge they need for the both of us – but what they do require is more discipline, help in sustaining better habits, being more strategic and acquiring the skills to make better decisions.

I once interviewed a lady who already had a coach but appeared to be getting nowhere fast. She came to see me for a second opinion and explained her frustration. She spoke very highly of her coach and noted her many years of coaching experience. Yet the thing that irritated her was the fact that she could never get a straight answer on anything and was so desperate for more candour in the relationship. After I'd made the necessary notes and before proposing a way forward, I did explain that Guerrilla Coaching was not about hand-holding nor was it counselling or simply offering lots of 'helpful advice'. However what I was willing to do was to create a coaching relationship where she and I would share the responsibility for all outcomes good, bad or indifferent. I could soon see a sparkle in her eyes and she asked if I would work with her. I did suggest going back to her current coach to request a different approach but she was adamant. In my experience very few clients want to generate all the solutions themselves and the vast majority seek a collaborative approach which is the fundamental principle of effective Guerrilla Coaching.

Third Legend: You can only be coached by one coach at a time

I was once contacted by the CEO of a well-known high street retail chain. Here was a guy at the top of his game, a millionaire many times over and one of the last people you may think would have the time or need for coaching. Yet there were a number of things that were bothering him and I soon appreciated that the challenge was more complex than I initially realised. He contacted me because he learned my unusual coaching style was very much about the speed of attaining results and he was looking for help to improve his flagging personal image in the press together with losing his growing introvert nature that was impacting upon his self confidence despite all that he had achieved to date. From the initial discussions I could see that there was a lot I could do for him through One to One coaching; but for maximum speed and biggest impact I thought I should enlist the help of two other colleagues with favoured specialities. One was an image consultant who also was a life coach and the other was a performance coach who created rapid self-confidence through a karate-based form of unarmed combat. My plan was to draft in all three of us in as a kind of 'Mission Impossible' team who would then coach the entrepreneur in a bespoke coaching package.

When I met him the second time to offer my proposal, I took my colleagues in with me and I could see he was a little taken aback by the three of us walking into his beautifully appointed office in the heart of London. Though somewhat cynical to begin with, after all here was I tripling the potential fee at a stroke, he realised my serious intent and so listened with interest at this unorthodox approach.

Over the years he had received coaching in various forms but never by three coaches all at the same time. This finally excited him sufficiently to arrive at a decision and at the end of the meeting he stuck his thumb in the air wanting to know when it would all commence. We ended up coaching him together and individually over a three-month period and I'm delighted to say he made new and important discoveries about himself that were essential in order for him to achieve new breakthroughs. This included his business as well as future aspirations in life as a whole. At the same time he had a complete image makeover and his wavering level of confidence suddenly soared being coached via the medium of unarmed combat. He subsequently changed his tailor, took up karate quite seriously and a two years later I heard he was nearing his brown belt at a time that was also being lauded by his shareholders.

Fourth Legend: Coaching is largely conducted in a room around a table

I met Myles Downey at a David Lloyd centre ready to play tennis. Or in my case I thought, *not to play tennis*. On the many previous occasions I had attempted to play the game I ended up embarrassing myself, so it was totally logical to be receiving some tennis coaching. The only thing that bothered me was this was booked as a business development session to fire up my new career as a coach. The fact was that I had no interest in improving my tennis whatsoever, but it soon became apparent that Myles was going to use tennis as a medium to get some deeper coaching principles across that I could use in all areas of my life as well as business. Myles started by looking down at my black trainers. "They may be a problem", he mused. This underlined the fact that I was light years from seeing myself as a serious tennis player. Once we got onto the court and had a knockabout almost instantly all my previous thoughts and memories about playing poor tennis came flooding back. I was soon embarrassing myself once more, with lots of seasoned tennis players buzzing around on the other courts making the experience even more painful. If this was coaching in humility then it was most certainly working. Myles then asked me to score myself out of 10 as to how good a tennis player I thought I was. Though the score came out at a mere 2 he smiled at me reassuringly. I was intrigued.

"Okay Glen what I'd like you to do are three things. When the ball comes over and you see it hit the deck shout BOUNCE. When your racket makes contact with the ball to return it, shout HIT. When you see the ball fly over the net and you think it's passing from your side to my side shout RETURN. Have you got that?"

It was as clear as a bell. I knew exactly what I had to do and without giving me any chance to think about it any further, the first ball was flying towards me like a meteor. I focused my attention carefully and at the point it hit the court I shouted 'bounce'! Then a few seconds later, noticing the ball had made contact with the racquet I shouted 'hit'! Finally as it went sailing over the net I looked carefully at the point at which it traversed from one side of the net to the other and bellowed 'return'!

What then transpired was quite extraordinary and I still remember it as if it only happened yesterday. Indeed it had a profound effect on me. Myles continued to play tennis as I went through my process of 'bounce-hit-return' on each rally, now completely neglecting to consider how poor a tennis player I perceived myself to be; a belief I had clung to since about the age of 10.

Only when I realised I was hitting and returning every single ball and what was actually going on was at odds with my belief did I once more miss the ball completely. Myles then called me to the net for a coaching conversation but just for a moment I was speechless because I also realised what I had been doing – I had outwitted my own mental chatter in playing tennis rather well.

"So how's that score doing?" smiled Myles.

"I think it's gone up to an 8!"

I realized that while focusing on three simple words I was

addressing the ball very effectively and playing tennis like a natural. Or should I say my subconscious was.

"An 8 did you say?" Myles shouted as he went back to the base line.

"Let's not stop now..."

Within seconds we back into another rally with me 'bounce, hit and returning' and dare I say soon getting quite cocky with my 'newly found' natural tennis skills, dug up from the deep caverns of my subconscious mind. I remember wishing I had the whole thing on video to show all my friends, yet the person who most needed to see it for all it was worth, was me.

Myles re-iterated that whenever we think of anything there's something that meets the edge of these thoughts called 'interference'. He explained it's exactly the same for catching a ball, skiing down a mountain or presenting to a large audience. If you believe you're not that good, then this will come through as mental chatter and more often than not sabotage how you perform. Yet if you distract these false beliefs, your performance improves immediately. Wow!

Perhaps the really cool thing I learned was that we are all '10' in say playing tennis and also have the potential in being '10' in skating, skiing, presenting or in fact any pursuit or activity you could possibly think of. The main saboteur invariably is *interference* and in coaching top tennis players or other sports professionals, one of the major strategies in the coaching package is dealing with that annoying, frustrating and often debilitating mental chatter that can decimate positive results at a stroke. This session with Myles typifies an important part of the Guerrilla Coaching style. About getting somebody to a personal breakthrough in the quickest possible time, in the most demonstrative way. Link this also with a location that will best achieve the learning or new level of performance. I would certainly have never got the same result or extraordinary insight in a tiny meeting room sitting around a table.

Fifth Legend: Coaching takes time to work

I recently met a musician who was keen to solicit my help. He had heard about Guerrilla Coaching and wondered if it could possibly apply it to his current goal. In his early twenties he was just starting out in the world and wanted to use his talents not just to teach music One-to-One, but also to get into television or media where all the fun seemed to be. I asked him to give me a very brief outline of where he was and what he wanted to achieve which he did very succinctly in three or four minutes. I then summarised it back to him. He was currently giving music lessons, charging relatively small sums and working on an hourly billing arrangement. His current challenge was where to get more clients from in order to fill up his rather empty diary. Then I volleyed a question which made him stop in his tracks. I simply asked him, 'why?'

He looked back as if I was an alien from Mars. "Why not? I want to build a business." I smiled and looked him directly. "Are you really telling me that this is what you want to do for the rest of your life? I thought you wanted to be a professional musician and appear on television?"

I noticed him rubbing his nose and then meekly responding that I was absolutely right. He did want to be a 'proper' musician but couldn't see how he could make the leap and do it full time or indeed be paid the kind of money that top musicians are paid when they become media stars.

This is one of the reasons why Guerrilla Coaching is not exclusively about having to fully rely on a template or model. My gut instinct was to challenge this guy and get him to improve his confidence and core beliefs while helping him to re-consider his goal completely. It would have been so easy to start working out a schedule of how he could pack more piano lessons into his empty diary, which is what he requested, yet engaging in this course of action would make me complicit in letting him down while instinctively knowing there had to be a better way. I looked at my notes and saw the pieces of the jigsaw emerging:

- Able musician
- Gives piano lessons
- Wants to be in television/media
- Low in confidence
- Danger of making situation worse

- Big paradigm about what he can and can't do
- Wants to break free and make it big

So I asked him to describe a typical music lesson, even though I didn't want to know about a typical music lesson at all. I actually wanted him to continue talking to me so I could surreptitiously observe visual clues whilst having a quick opportunity to fully consider the pieces of the jigsaw one last time. Again may I stress that Guerrilla coaching is about a fifty-fifty shared commitment between you and your client. As far as I was concerned the client relationship had already started quite regardless of whether he wanted to ultimately hire me or not. I was on the case and getting a strong feeling in my stomach that prompted me to ask, "Any music?"

My comment made no sense given he was at the point of explaining how he introduces sheet music into early lessons. So he looked up a little confused. I repeated my question:

"Can you teach any type of music?"

He proceeded to give me a long list of all the styles of music he was very confident in teaching that were all largely classical.

"What about Elton John?"

Though feeling like I was showing my age in front of this twenty-something. I couldn't stop now and even named a song:

"Rocket Man."

"Erm, yes I think so."

"What's the shortest time you could have me playing Rocket Man?"

"How much experience do you have in playing piano?"

"None."

"I'm not sure. You'll need to be able to read sheet music, so a good couple of years perhaps."

"How long?" I over did a gasp on purpose.

"Okay, eighteen months maybe."

"Too long. I'd get bored."

For the next six minutes I started to challenge him on all his paradigms to the point at which I asked him an ultimate guerrilla style question: "If your life depended on it, how quickly could you get me to play 'Rocket Man?' I'm serious. Remember, if life itself depended on it."

There was an extremely long pause before his answer.

"Six weeks."

"What if I didn't have six weeks and I only had 30 days? And I paid you £1,000 a day for each of those 30 days?"

He suddenly beamed. "No problem. When do you want to start?"

I sat back in my chair with a big grin as I watched him realise what he'd just said. I call this an *immediate outcome*.

I like to think that this musician left our very brief discovery session, which lasted a mere 26 minutes, a new man. He had a spring in his step and an amazing idea buzzing around his mind that had already turned his 'known world' completely upside down. The idea of being able to sell a brand new product that would have an infinitely higher financial value compared with teaching traditional-thinking students their music scales was a real breakthrough he wasn't expecting but was now savouring.

I knew at this point that whether we met again or not, I had already coached him. I even caught myself thinking about signing up for a 30-day package with him. (Though I would perhaps need to re-negotiate the price a tad.)

Sixth Legend: Coaching requires at least an hour per session

In my early career I tended to set aside quite large chunks of time for coaching , a habit I had picked up from life coach Roger Stedman who ran his own brand of coaching called 'Life Plan'. Sessions were at least three hours and sometimes four. He once invited me to have a session with him and though I did benefit from the coaching enormously, the session felt far too long. Equally, in my own coaching sessions in the early days I did sense that breakthroughs with clients were being lost by putting too many layers on to the coaching cake.

Three years ago, I met a colleague who I'd worked with on and off over the years called Jonathan Streeton. We actually met in Bettys Tea Room at Harrogate close to where he lived. As we caught up with various ideas on the future of our respective consultancies, I shared the results of a little experiment I had carried out with a handful of my best business clients. I explained this new idea called 'Carpe Diem' the Latin for 'Seize the Day'. The concept was extremely simple: each day my client would ring me for a strictly 7-minute call where they would share three goals for that day that I would follow up on in their next 7-minute contact with me. The goals would be an Essential Goal, a Reluctant or Stretch Goal and a 'Champagne' Goal. The goals would carry a percentage rating where the Essential goal was worth 15%, the Reluctant goal 25% and the 60% balance went to the Champagne one. There would also be a more strategic call that lasted 16 minutes giving four 7-minute calls and one 16-minute call each week. Jonathan went very quiet as he made various notes and I initially thought that he was being very polite while really thinking I had lost my marbles. Then he suddenly declared that he liked the idea very much and would like to put it to the test with some major brands he was currently working with. These included Nokia, Energizer, L'Oreal, Shell and Dairy Crest. With each of these companies. I would coach one of their senior guys which typically would be a sales director or senior account manager. One month later the results were out and both Jonathan and I were stunned. Without exception every single manager found the process challenging, insightful, inspirational but most of all it helped them to be more successful in less time. This was the birth of the world's first 7-Minute Coaching System and since then we have continued our work with other very well-known companies, building a small team of 'Carpe Diem' coaches at the same time.

Today in a Facebook/Twitter world where people are keen to get to the heart of the matter rapidly, a fast approach is an obvious must. Delivering coaching in just 7 minutes each business day, normally before 9am required some specially designed software accompanied by audio and video media with a competent coach behind it. However when you pull all these strings together there's no question that people appreciate that impact with brevity delivered in a compelling way leverages phenomenal coaching results. Clients soon noticed that they were getting far more from this approach compared with the longer more traditional executive coaching sessions that could often run for hours each month. As ever, I'm not suggesting that one method supersedes another but when coaching in today's brave new world there are lots of other options to consider depending on who you're coaching, what their objectives are and how quickly they want to reach the promised land.

Seventh Legend: Coaching is normally a defined number of sessions

Most coaching proposals define a number of sessions or calendar months as part of the structure. For example, three, six, nine or twelve month packages are quite common. You could also take the view that if you're only going to coach someone for a predetermined period what happens after that? Yes, you could extend the coaching and it really all depends what the goals are. My approach has always been about creating an on-going relationship where the client raises their hand when they feel that they've had enough. Counter balancing this philosophy is about giving immense value as there's little point of coach and coachee regularly working together yet rarely achieving anything new. But here's a potential contradiction: speedy results versus longevity of the client relationship. I humbly suggest you that you can have both. Sessions can feature rapid results yet on an on-going basis. I have one client who has been with me for over 12 years now whilst others get all they require in a couple of sessions. Ultimately the means of measurement has to be stated goals compared with desired results.

Eighth Legend: People who can, do – people who can't, coach

There could be an element of truth in the above for some coaches but there's always the stronger counter-argument that for example, some of the best tennis coaches in the world, have never played tennis competitively before. It's also a bit like running a business that's all about helping other businesses to succeed. If the business that's helping other businesses succeed is successful itself, do you applaud that business or sneer at it cynically?

There's no doubt that the biggest challenge for most coaches is 'to walk the walk'. Okay, we are all human and have our frailties; we tend to capitalise on our strengths and hide our weaknesses. Rather than doing the latter, it's always good to be aware of what you perceive yourself as not good at and at the very least, find someone who can help you overcome what is most likely to be a psychological obstacle. Here is where a good coach is worth their weight. It takes a certain process to coach and not everyone is prepared to master it for the benefit of others. This means that successful coaches have mastered a special set of skills and achievement principles in their own right. They are the catalyst in a chemical reaction that produces a big bright spark. No catalyst, no reaction, no sparkling outcome. But does the coach have to sign up to a set of principles themselves in order to do this? I believe they do.

Any principle, concept or guerrilla tactic I offer, I will have experienced or used myself in order that I'm not simply passing on a theory that I've taken from thin air. If the tool doesn't work for me yet works for lots of others I may still recommend it provided my client knows my own lack of success with it.

The other aspect about being acknowledged as an achiever in your own right is the client's perception of you as a skilled practitioner. Would you engage a gym trainer who was a heavy smoker and grossly overweight? What about a life coach who was in a similar situation? Coaches don't have to be super-heros or angels, though I would have doubts about a hiring a coach who preached the importance of discipline and the power of transformation who was unable to apply it to their own health. (Those who can't do, coach).

Some coaches who I have approached on this subject often say that they "choose to smoke" or "like to be overweight." All I can say is that I find it very hard to accept that we are talking about anything other than the application of personal discipline. If the person persisted in convincing me that it was choice rather than discipline over anything that seriously threatened their health then I would see them as quite simply fooling themselves.

One of my previous clients, Sandro Forte, is probably the most successful international keynote speaker in financial services. He's a shining example of someone who walks the walk. Not only does he inspire large audiences to do business more successfully, but at the same time he's also running an extremely successful commercial enterprise in its own right. What he coaches he uses and what he uses makes him successful. The most impressive quality as a coachee that I remember was his unquestioning application of any tool or technique that I strongly recommended he use. He would simply get his head around how it worked and then deploy it until it did. Consequently he went from good to great in a very short space of time and a handful of coaching sessions.

Ninth Legend: You have to be qualified to be a coach

Of course you do, though qualifications come in different forms, and the more qualifications you're prepared to spend time attaining the better for sure. The myth perhaps is holding up paper qualifications in place of experience and ability. If you are qualifying to be a doctor, you will appreciate that over eighty percent of your learning will be entirely practical to give you real experience along with your paper degree. So any coach worth their salt will be lapping up as much experience as they can alongside their professional learning. There's also a lot to be said for hands on practical experience being the most important qualification of all.

Taking Stock

So it's time to really roll our sleeves up and look at Guerrilla Coaching more closely. If I manage to help just one coach improve their game and in turn help a single coachee succeed in something they earnestly desire, perhaps beyond their wildest dreams, then all of this will have been worthwhile.

2

GUERRILLA COACHING UNZIPPED

As a coach, I wonder what your key frustrations are? In a moment I will share my original list of frustrations, many of which disappeared as soon as I made a point of seeking out solutions. One such early solution came in the form of 3 simple changes to my coaching style recommended by a more experienced practitioner at the time. These were:

- Be more candid with your client
- Put intuition first, and any coaching model second
- Remind your client that both parties reserve the right to stop the coaching

In hindsight I appreciate that these top 3 tips were to form the foundations of my future approach with clients.

The £200 Cheque

The first piece of true 'guerrilla DNA' came twenty years ago when I was working with a senior board director of a well-known company. He had been introduced to me through a friend of a friend, and was sampling 'executive coaching' for the first time. Simon was 46 and a busy man who desperately wanted to achieve more from the time he had available each week, balanced with an equally hectic home life. This was the third session and from my perspective I was a little disappointed that after the first and second sessions he had failed to keep the commitments he'd readily agreed to.

As he entered the room this time, he was expressionless as he placed his leather briefcase to one side and then looked at me a little nervously. My first question was a straightforward yet a very important one. I had to know whether he'd kept the commitments he made at the last meeting. I could soon see his eyes moving elsewhere, avoiding all contact with me. Though I waited for his response I knew what he was about to say, and then almost on cue, he said it:

"I'm sorry I didn't have time to complete..." He paused, then added "my homework." I mused on his choice of words. This instantly took me back to my youth and felt myself observing a naughty schoolboy who had signed up to complete a task and promptly ignored the whole thing once he had exited the school gates.

"So what happened?"

"I just got caught up on a few things and I couldn't do anything about it. Totally out of my control I'm afraid."

There was that thought going through my head as to how ineffective a coach I had been with this particular client. Surely if I was competent we wouldn't be having this conversation and he would have bounced in with the great news of what he'd achieved. Since this hadn't happened, I was rapidly concluding that the fault lay entirely in my lap and I was trying to reassess the best course of action to rescue my professional reputation. Then a much stronger thought came to me quite spontaneously, and I started to go down a different track that turned out to be a big surprised to both my client ...and myself.

"Do you have your cheque book with you?" I enquired.

"How do you mean?"

"Your cheque book. Is it in your briefcase?"

I looked at him squarely between the eyes.

"As a matter of fact it is, why?"

"I'd like you to get it out and write a cheque for £200 to somebody who you'd hate to send the money to."

There was a silence as he tried to make sense of what I was saying, and even I was half-asking myself: "Where am I going with this exactly?"

Just before he had time to query it any further I decided to clarify the position.

"Is there someone right now who you'd hate to send a cheque for £200 to? And please play along with me for the moment." I smiled reassuringly which probably made it all the more confusing. Assuming that this was some coaching exercise he replied:

"Yes, my mother-in-law."

I then proceeded to suggest that if he were to provide me with a cheque made out to his mother-in-law for £200, if he failed to keep his commitments between today and the next session, I would mail the cheque to her to the address that he would write on the back. It took me a good twenty minutes to get him to agree to seriously go through with his bizarre request. He started by giving me every excuse under the sun as to why this was totally unnecessary and all rather silly, however when I stressed that he would get the cheque back provided he kept his word, he had to reluctantly agree that if he was serious this time, why wouldn't he want to hand over the cheque? And rather like a clip from 'Who Wants To Be A Millionaire' he had one hand on the left side of the cheque with my hand on the right side and we had a last minute tug-of-war until I pulled it in my direction and grasped it with both hands. I then continued with the session having pinned the cheque to the inside of his file.

A couple of weeks went by and Simon returned for his next session. I was very much looking forward to this, given the somewhat unorthodox guerrilla tactics I had used in the last meeting. Once again he walked in with his leather briefcase, put it at the side of the armchair and plonked himself down in a somewhat unceremonious fashion. I instantly evaluated that there was something amiss given his crooked tie and open shirt, yet I offered a welcoming smile and waited for him to speak first.

"I suppose you're wondering how I did with my list of commitments?"

"Absolutely."

"I'm afraid I failed miserably. I just didn't have enough time again. Sorry."

"Did you do any of them?" I asked inwardly wincing.

"I'm afraid not."

I then opened the file and prised out the cheque for £200 duly signed with his mother-in-law's name and address on the back, immediately rose to my feet and with the cheque in my firm grasp explained that I was about to take it through to my secretary who would then put it in today's post. What was worrying me though was the fact that he wasn't reacting at all and so I repeated quite clearly what I was about to do, and he just nodded passively.

"So you're quite happy for me to send this cheque off then?"

"You can if you want", he replied, now betraying a slight smirk. My mind was racing, as I tried to decipher what was going on here. And then quite suddenly and totally out of the blue he said:

"You see on the way here I went by my bank and stopped the cheque."

I'm not sure what possessed me to say the next thing yet it came out of my mouth like a high-speed train from a dark tunnel.

"Great, and I've just stopped the coaching."

As I deliberated as to whether that was an appropriate or professional response, there was a long marked silence in the room as no doubt he was now trying to make sense of what was unfolding here.

"What do you mean?"

"Simon that's the end of the coaching, I'm really sorry."

"You can't get rid of me. I'm a client."

"Were a client. Did you bring a coat?"

I must confess that I didn't actually say the last part about the coat, though that's what I wanted to add.

A speedy back-peddling conversation ensued as he finally concluded that he'd definitely learned something from 'the exercise' and apologised for his inappropriate behaviour in stopping off at the bank. He was now prepared to put 'his all' into the next month's commitments.

I firmly believe that this was the first time I'd ever used a guerrilla tactic like this one and it would have been so easy to have simply accepted his apology and carried on as if nothing had happened and yet I couldn't. It didn't seem right. I felt as if I would be reneging on my own integrity so I decided that I was not going to change my mind and if it was only one of us was able to keep their commitment then it had to be me, the coach.

Eventually he picked up his briefcase and shook my hand quite firmly before leaving. I never saw him again though I did speak to him that afternoon on the call he put into me to try and convince me to continue the coaching. Once again I turned him down politely and it was the last connection we ever had.

I can say that it wasn't a complete disaster because after a few months I heard how well he had done in his company following the last coaching session with me! It was clear that our interaction had indeed played a big part in this because I ended up getting a stream of enquiries over the years from people that he knew who were looking for an effective coach. After the £200 cheque incident, I began to take commitments in coaching even more seriously with everyone I worked with. What was the point of going through a process where the word 'commitment' was used and then promptly discarded. It made a complete mockery of the whole process. I began to realize that by limply accepting client excuses and politely suggesting they try again next time, I was being complicit in their lack of respect for themselves. Some excuses are acceptable of course and I am not suggesting that guerrilla coaching is about being heartless, yet it is true that the majority of reasons for not following through are invariably unacceptable and this fact cannot be brushed under the carpet.

If you think about it, the idea of being able to state what you want as a goal, then go out and attain it without any effort whatsoever, each and every time, would be amazing. If we were all able to do this in our personal/business lives, there would be no requirement for coaching of any kind. The reality is of course very different. We live in a world where all of us as individuals, families, groups and businesses desire to achieve regular sets of objectives whether as personal challenges or simple economic necessities. The benefit of a worthy coach, is to help you to do whatever it takes; support you to leverage the difference that makes a difference and help you identify exactly what's required to propel you over the all important finishing line. This is guerrilla coaching at its best, helping clients attain the best results at maximum speed, always aiming for over-achievement rather than merely hitting the target.

My Other Key Frustrations in Coaching

1 The client doesn't seem to want to connect with me
2 The client hasn't 'bought-in' to the coaching
3 I am not sure how best to help my client
4 I feel I lack specialist knowledge
5 I have failed to impress the client in the first session
6 I've done a good job so far but the client doesn't want to continue
7 The client is just not improving or achieving any of their goals
8 The client feels better but there is no tangible evidence of results
9 The client is being skeptical/negative
10 The client takes things with a pinch of salt
11 The client fails to keep agreed commitments
12 The client is not returning my calls promptly

All of these challenges will be dealt with in more detail in Chapter 9, meanwhile I'd like to suggest that if you are having a hard time with some of these 'gremlins', you might like to consider using one or all three of my previous 'top 3 tips' because I think you'll be pleasantly surprised at what these changes in approach will bring to your coaching, that is of course if you're not already using them.

Putting You on the Spot

Now I have a question for you. Imagine you've been approached by a client who's desperate to be coached. In an initial informal exploratory meeting you find out that they're about to embark upon part-time study with the Open University and want to ensure that they pass their Arts Foundation course with flying colours in the allotted twelve months. So over to you, how would you help them? I'd like you to do this exercise for real. In the space provided, please make some instant notes based on the very little information you have been given. I fully appreciate that you may have a million questions you'd like to ask this person, however go for it anyway. After you've finished, have a look at my suggestions.

Case History: Brian Harris

Coaching objective: To pass their Arts Foundation Course at the Open University in 12 months

Challenges outlined: Lack of confidence in studying, perceived poor memory, never passed many exams at school, low self-esteem around studying and attaining qualifications.

Suggested Solution:

What I am about to list may appear to be just a bunch of ideas but I want to assure you that they are part of a coaching process based on *The Guerrilla Wheel*. We are to explore the wheel in more detail, but for now please accept that the wheel contains coaching strategies that include 6 Interventions or coaching area options to be covered in Chapter 3.

The ones I decided to use were: *Mindset, Performance, Self-Discovery* and *Set Skills*.

It was the last intervention Set Skills that I had to do a little research around because although I had an idea of some study techniques already, I wanted to ensure any skill I was about to offer would make a genuine difference with a proven track record. The interventions around mindset, performance and self-discovery would underpin these skills, hopefully giving my client maximum confidence in using his new 'study toolkit' to full advantage.

Brian's Master Plan

My suggestion was to have weekly sessions with a monthly follow-up call. Because this was a personal friend I was very happy he contact me at any time if he was really struggling at any point. Each coaching session would last 45 minutes. The first was to be on the terrace of a beautiful Georgian manor hotel in Coventry not far from Warwick University that was a perfect location for the time of year whilst being psychologically anchored with a respected 'seat of learning'.

I ensured that the coaching was largely experiential, starting with the all-important mindset element. Each session flew by but I'm delighted to report that Brian got tremendous value from the coaching. I also made sure that I e-mailed a summary of session points immediately after each 'face to face' which was waiting for him when he got home.

Here is a very brief overview of the strategy I suggested:

- Explore mindset and reasonbs for study plus what success would mean longer term.

- Ascertaining all of Brian's existing methods of learning and note taking and how to build on the successful ones. Also checking and confirming what his preferred learning style was and how we best use this to his advantage. (Brian turned out to be a 'high-visual').

- The use of mind maps for study and note taking. The idea was to ensure a mind map existed for every important piece of information or essay alongside any linear notes.

- Six of the best ways to take notes in a lecture or tutorial. This offered additional ideas on note taking where wide margins with key words, colour and line drawings created a much more visually appealing and easier-to-remember studying process.

- Key index cards – simple, easy and effective. Brian was to make key notes on index cards on all his main subjects and every day look through the set just once. By the time the exams arrived the chances are he would have committed most of it to memory from the regular habit of daily review.

- The Memory Peg System – a quick way of being able to remember lists of things in a highly effective manner. Fortunately because of Brian's visual sensory preference this helped him a great deal.

- Twenty suggestions for passing exams more effectively. This I found on the Internet from a respected source and I downloaded the document which was packed full of goodies. Some of the tools I was aware of and had used myself; others were brand new. During the coaching I ensured Brian knew the ones I could recommend from experience and the ones that he may have to experiment.

- The use of recorded audio-files that he could transfer to his phone or other mobile device and listen to when commuting to and from work on the train.

The approach I took with Brian followed a guerilla methodology that I am looking forward to expanding upon. It started with "For now I'd like to ask you how you did with coaching tools and ideas?" Of course there is no right or wrong answer. The most important thing for me was that Brian went on to achieve his objectives. He was to subsequently report that the biggest win for him was that he suddenly began to thoroughly enjoy studying for the first time ever. He found it much easier to remember information and his level of self-confidence in continuing with the OU and an honours degree went from a 'low' to a big thumbs up 'high'. What I can confidently report in this case history is that I made the coaching as palatable as possible and intriguing enough at the outset for Brian to want to pick up the ball and run. He was the one who ultimately did all the hard work though the coaching provided a much needed catalyst to push him away from worry and forward to action.

The 'Genius Myth' in Guerrilla Coaching

It's fascinating to see people's associations with the word 'genius'. Could it be that this word has been embellished and overly animated to produce an extremely misleading concept? It's gratifying to see that scientists and psychologists have no unified position on what genius is within the Human Race. As a coach, I'm very certain that my understanding of this word will completely affect how successful I will be in coaching and developing others. Particularly in terms of how much success the coachee will ultimately achieve and enjoy.

When looking up the dictionary definition, a genius is apparently *someone embodying exceptional intellectual ability, creativity or originality*. It goes on to say that a genius is associated with the ability of unprecedented insight. When you ask most people to name a genius the number one answer is normally Albert Einstein followed by people like Thomas Edison, Leonardo da Vinci and Mozart. (I think Shakespeare has a look-in on this 'celeb' list too.) Yet if you were in a position to be able to ask any of these people whether they considered themselves as geniuses, the chances are none would raise their hand and say, "Yep, that's me."

So is genius merely a perception? Not according to most psychologists. What most do agree on, is that genius may be found in a whole variety of pursuits such as mathematics, music, literature, art, science and so on. Genius is also cited as an extreme form of originality.

So here's a completely different take on genius that I would like to throw into the ring: genius as it's perceived by most of us is a complete myth. It's an excuse we love to use to describe other people in order that we don't have to follow in their footsteps and potentially fail. It's a label we want to pin on people who have intuitively chosen to be top of their game, while being completely original and passionate about the exceptional direction they've chosen to pursue.

Was Wolfgang Mozart a genius? I do not believe so. Interesting how he was taught music by his father, Leopold Mozart who was a music teacher coupled with the fact that young Wolfgang also had a real passion for music at a very early age. He also came from a rich family who could afford a piano, and he pursued music because it gave him immense pleasure. Follow the same principles with a youngster today who's really into computers say, or indeed buy one for them at an early age and you too may well have an IT genius on your hands if they enjoy themselves in this pursuit. In short, if Mozart was a genius then we all are. Every human has genius potential within them. They are born that way. Every potential client I meet I perceive as oozing with genius abilities that I would like to help them realise.

You can imagine some of the conversations I've had with highly qualified psychologists who say I have no idea what I'm talking about. Perhaps they're right, but who would you rather coach you to achieve something immensely challenging or ambitiious? Someone who has immediately written you off as not having genius capability, or someone who passionately believes in the natural genius within you and is equally passionate about helping you release the potential as quickly as possible?

In the end, I don't really care what 'the facts' are about genius. As a coach committed to the success of others, as well as my own, I am more than happy to create a powerful, positive paradigm if need be that genius is within us all and we only have to tap into it. This strategy has created more successful clients for me over the years, many of whom report back the use of the word 'genius' to describe their endeavours by others.

I remember meeting a friend from school who I had not seen for a long while by the name of Tracey. In our catch-up conversation she mentioned how she'd been to a karaoke evening but unfortunately wasn't able to participate. When I enquired further she made a casual comment that quickly got my attention. She said, "Glen, the problem is that I'm tone deaf." When I pressed her for more information she reminded me that when we were at school aged 11 our music teacher had told her to stand to one side during some singing auditions because she was tone deaf and would never make it as a singer.

After hearing the whole story I smiled and came back to her with a poignant two-part question:

"But would you like to sing?" and "What difference would being able to sing well make to you?"

As you may well imagine her whole face beamed and her eyes lit up all be it momentarily. It was obvious she had a deep desire for the dream of singing her heart out yet had been convinced at an early age that it just wasn't possible in her case. When I went on to confirm that 'tone deaf' was not a medical condition and is quite simply someone's personal opinion, I got her immediately re-evaluating her beliefs. I then proceeded to suggest how our music teacher had merely given her own opinion, and if she had been worth her weight as a more competent teacher, she would have done something positive to coach Tracey to discover the genius that she was undoubtedly born with.

After much persuasion I managed to get my old school friend to meet a singing coach. After just one single session a package arrived in the post which was a cassette tape featuring Tracey finally singing her heart out. I have to admit that as I listened I got quite emotional because not only was her voice outstanding but I could hear the immense joy in her passionate delivery.

Without delay I picked up the phone to congratulate her.

Yet her response was initially surprising as she said that she felt betrayed and was quite angry. "My music teacher robbed me of at least 15 years of the joy of singing because I had believed her when she told me the lie that I was tone deaf."

There are numerous examples I can cite how as a coach, I've done the opposite to what the misguided music teacher had probably done to many of her unfortunate students. The starting point is freeing the genius within the mind of the client like setting free a genie in a bottle.

Similarly, I remember having a conversation with my first accountant in the 1980s who candidly expressed his desire to write a children's book, though said he lacked confidence to do anything about it. After some rapid on the spot coaching he went away with a completely different set of beliefs about getting published and a few months later told me about his first book contract. I believe since that time he has written at least 20 or 30 books, many of which are selling all over the world.

My favourite example though Is Ian Willoughby, who was a financial adviser I was coaching in the '90s. He was pleased with how things were going with the help I was offering in business coaching, yet in an unguarded moment an interesting truth popped out. He told me of an ambition he had from early childhood about becoming a pilot. When I suggested that there should be no problem whatsoever in taking some flying lessons to get his private pilot's licence, he looked at me awkwardly and explained that the kind of plane he wanted to fly was a jumbo jet!

Since I love a challenge, I threw down the gauntlet immediately. I dared him to pursue his dream as far as he could possibly take it, to which he gladly accepted, all credit to him. He was aware too that his age would probably go against him and after initial calls to airlines this was confirmed. They would almost laugh down the phone when he said he was in his late thirties. The cut-off age was around 23.

Over the years to come he did things like remortgage his house, go to foreign lands for lessons that were too expensive in the UK, and eventually he came back with a commercial pilot's licence. However the worst was yet to come as he was now told that he didn't have sufficient flying hours. The challenges kept coming thick and fast, but like a jockey determined to win the ultimate prize in the Grand National, he squeezed himself into the saddle of his dreams and refused to be knocked down.

Today Ian Willoughby flies for British Airways, his dream airline and indeed the one he mentioned in that original coaching session we had when I teased out of him this 'blue sky' thinking. Curious isn't it that he was once described by a flight instructor as having a real genius for flying.

All of this could possibly be described as a 'Placebo Effect'. What makes me smile is when someone says that the only reason they got better was because they were given a placebo, it's as if a cure by this method doesn't count! Time and time again people get well because they are given a tablet which has no medicinal value, yet their belief in the tablet is enough to affect a cure through their mind.

Whatever we choose to believe, whatever we lock into our 'Belief System' as true is nearly always likely to become our final stark reality.

At seven years old I was in the school playground and I noticed a boy using a pin from a lifeboat badge that he had stuck through his finger. As I stared carefully in amazement I could actually see the pin going through his skin and he stood there just smiling. Given that seeing is nearly always believing, I decided I wanted to have a go at this and I found someone else with a lifeboat pin. Not realising that he'd used the quite ordinary pin through the top surface of his skin where there are no nerves and therefore no pain, I was really going for it pushing the pin in a lot deeper into my finger yet also achieving the same objective, despite the fact my finger was also getting rather red and wet at the same time. What I do remember even to this day is I felt no pain whatsoever. Indeed the only point at which it did hurt was when a dinner lady rescued me with her handkerchief explaining that what I was doing was not the same as what the other boy had done. As soon as I realised the difference, my finger hurt like hell. Children are probably the most open minded human beings of all and as we grow older many windows of our once wide open minds start shutting down. The good news is that the process can be reversed and with the right coaching and tools one's age is irrelevant.

All these takes on 'genius' are for you to make your own mind up as to where you are on this critical path at a coaching crossroads. Some coaches will stay traditional and say that you can measure IQ, therefore genius is a reality, others like me will say that I can help someone improve their IQ score by coaching them on taking IQ tests – which partly makes the testing process a nonsense and therefore genius is not just about IQ.

Whether you know which path you wish to follow in coaching and given this book is written in notebook style, I have a couple more examples I would like you to be aware of.

Swimming is one of them.

It's a fact that every human swims at birth. Indeed the best time to take your newborn swimming is at six weeks old. I've actually watched swimming trainers who take babies of that age and 'whoosh' them on the surface of three feet of water. The baby literally skips along the water's surface, disappears and re-emerges floating on his or her back in a kind of swimming motion. We've probably all seen babies swimming under water with their parents on television before. There are many adverts that use this wonderful imagery which is fantastic to watch. The baby always has a big smile and also knows when it's time for some more air. One of the main reasons there are non-swimmers in the world is because parents come along and suggest a not-being-able-to-swim-idea in the first place to an impressionable mind.

Someone once asked me why he wasn't able to sing operatically if he was born an opera singer as I was suggesting. I was able to deal with this quite simply:

"Do you want to be an opera singer?"

"No"

"Then that's the reason. If you woke up tomorrow with a real

desire to sing opera and were really passionate about it, then your ability would improve immediately."

"I don't think so."

"What if you were offered a million pounds to be a competent opera singer in 30 days?" (You already know where I'm going with this).

"That's mad."

"No, seriously what if I did?"

After a pause and a smile he replied: "I see your point."

And of course it's not always about money, it's about what drives us to accept certain beliefs and dismiss others.

Doctor Gets Struck by Lightning

In 1994, when Tony Cicoria, a qualified doctor, was 42 years old, he was struck by lightning near Albany, New York, while standing next to a public telephone. He had just hung up the phone and was about a foot away when a rogue bolt of lightning struck the phone booth. He recalled seeing his own body on the ground surrounded by a bluish-white light. Cicoria's heart had apparently stopped, but he was resuscitated by a woman, who happened to be an intensive-care nurse waiting to use the telephone.

Then Cicoria, over a period of two or three days, became struck with an insatiable desire to listen to piano music. He acquired a piano and started to teach himself to play. His head was flooded with music that seemed to come from nowhere. Although, previous to his accident, he had no particular interest in music, within three months of being a lightning conductor Cicoria spent nearly all his spare time playing and composing on the piano.

Tony Cicoria debuted his first piano composition in Westport, Connecticut, on October 12, 2007, under the direction of Polly van der Linde, to a discerning audience. Since then he has given recitals at the Sonata Adult Piano Camp, in Bennington, Vermont, where he has played Chopin's *Military Polonaise*, Chopin's *Fantasie-Impromptu*, Brahms' *Rhapsody*, Chopin's *Scherzo in B-flat Minor, Op. 31* and an earlier version of his own composition, *Lightning Sonata*.

Can you believe this?

This true story staggers the imagination and confounds science and psychology, yet is so pivotal to who we all truly are if only we realised. We have so many hidden talents, skills and abilities that are there within us all, and in Cicoria's case, one was prized out of him in a bizarre accident that changed his life forever.

Introducing the Guerrilla Wheel

Origin of the Wheel

Before technology brought us things like the iPad and wafer-thin laptops, there was always good old-fashioned pencil and paper and for a fair number of years I carried around a large ring binder notebook where I'd mind map notes for each coaching session using coloured pens in a landscape format.

As I collected all these ring binders, I began to review them and see a pattern emerging in the way I was planning and executing coaching sessions. There was always the choice of location high on my agenda followed by the creation of some sort of Master Plan while working with the client. Then consideration was given to which 'interventions' or coaching areas I should consider focusing on with the implementation of specific levers that would fast track results. Wherever possible sessions would be as short as possible with some practical or experiential element to them.

Finally I noticed that I would take opportunities to think, coach and create a template that took account of as many of the five senses as possible due to my experience and knowledge of neuro-linguistics. Out of all of this eventually emerged *The Guerrilla Wheel* which has worked wonders for clients and something I'm now proud to share with you.

If you imagine the subconscious mind to be housed in a safe, and in order to gain access and communicate with it, you would need to discover the right combination, then, every human would probably have their own unique combination.

In The Guerrilla Wheel I identified 7 'Tumblers'.

Wikipedia describes a tumbler as: *A part of a lock whose position must be changed by a key in order to release the bolt and gain access.*

In the wheel I imagined that there were tumblers or triggers that once chosen, may be placed in a sequence that would best suit the client. So when you look at the wheel, the fact that Speed is number 1 and Interventions is number 2 and so on is to give you the word 'SIMILES' which is an acronym to help remember what the 7 Tumblers are. In fact these seven coaching devices may be used in any order and you don't have to use all of them.

Since the word 'tumbler' refers to the device within the combination mechanism in a safe, get the tumbler choice and order of their use right and the safe opens. Hopefully you see the analogy here.

What I can report is that the more tumblers you are able to use in coaching sessions the better the result appears to be.

When I first shared The Guerrilla Wheel with other coaches for the first time, the immediate question was how it would fit with well known coaching models like GROW for example. I'm delighted to confirm that The Guerrilla Wheel can work in perfect harmony with any model or process because it's designed to embellish and enhance rather than replace or remove. I'm obviously biased, and use The

Guerrilla Wheel as my primary coaching mechanism when guerrilla coaching. In planning a session, provided I have taken account of all 7 Tumblers, I'm confident that the session will have the desired impact with the depth of inspiration essential to stimulate my coachee into committing to a set of goals that will have every chance of leading to one hundred percent achievement.

Chapters 3 to 9 explore each tumbler individually.

Overview of the 7 Tumblers

The First Tumbler – Speed

This tumbler is all about doing more in less time. If we consider a 'face to face', a true guerrilla session should be around 45 minutes or less. If you think about it, the optimum time for a TV show is 30-60 minutes. (A one hour show is often 45 minutes without adverts). A show less than 30 minutes can make the audience feel unsatisfied, while a show that goes on for over an hour better be a really good one because many people may have already switched TV channel. Similarly with coaching sessions, impetus may be lost by slowing everything down over too much time and spending up to three hours with a client is not recommended. Better short sessions more regularly rather than one long one each month. Speed also refers to the attainment of *immediate outcomes*.

The Second Tumbler – Interventions

The second segment of The Guerrilla Wheel is about Interventions or coaching areas and there are six to choose from with any client. There have been comments from coaches who ask where leadership is for example. Leadership straddles all of these categories ranging from mindset, strategy, performance to self-discovery, creativity and set skills within that topic. Within each type of intervention sits a whole range of coaching tools and devices and at the last count my full list numbered 94. Although it would take a longer book to offer all of them, I will offer you a fair few in Chapter 6: The Coaching Vault.

The Third Tumbler – Master Plan

As the words suggest, there is only one if it's a Master Plan, so this isn't with reference to a master plan for each session. In a first session it would be important to create the basis of an on going future horizon, scanner screen or Master Plan. In subsequent sessions client and coach can come back to it to add, subtract or review in order to ensure the overall direction is still the right one.

The Fourth Tumbler – Implementation

This is about the use of specific results-focused tools to help take the appropriate action that will lead clients to the promised land. Implementation is also about sustaining success between coaching sessions, or the next contact by telephone.

To be crystal clear, the difference between *levers* and *tools* is as follows: A lever is one of 7 methods I've identified to create a quick win or *immediate outcome*. A tool however is part of an endless number of devices that are part of any coach's tooolkit for ongoing use when coaching. In time there will be other levers I am sure, but for now there are just seven. I will expand upon this presently.

The Fifth Tumbler – Location

Choosing where you coach your client can make an enormous difference to the feeling and mood of the session, not to mention the potential inspirational impact on your client. What's also worth thinking about is how to change the location for each 'face to face' regardless, so that any associations with a particular session isn't automatically applied to the second, third, or fourth session, unless this is what you desire. From a location perspective I would also strongly advise you to avoid coaching in a client's office, personal workspace or even your own office. There are usually too many of the wrong associations coupled with these somewhat expected locations.

The Sixth Tumbler – Experiential

This is probably preaching to the converted and isn't it important that your client has some practical/experiential action in each coaching session? Part of creating that experience is the words and phrases you use and the way you use them. This would also apply to your delivery style, tone of voice, volume at which you speak and the speed of your delivery.

What will you say and how will you say it to get your client up on their feet so they take more responsibility and action in the session for example?

The Seventh Tumbler – Sensory

Do consider the importance of taking full account of all five senses when coaching. Most coaches are aware of the importance of identifying the sensory preference of a client, but I suggest going further and ensuring you get as many of the five senses into the session itself. Walking into a location with a great view, mural visuals, music playing, coffee being filtered, food items to nibble and a comfy seat to sit on is one example of the basic 5-Sense Experience. Be creative and ensure there is a strong, positive and lasting association for the session that the client's subconscious takes away and re-plays many times.

The 7 Guerrilla Levers – more information

So if you have a Guerrilla Wheel to play with that gives you a steer towards session content/structure and some guerrilla coaching values that will also become apparent to guide you, why would you need anything else?

Well if the wheel is the map on your coaching journey, the values 'your compass', then the levers are essential items in your ruck sack that you may need soonest like a sleeping bag, torch, spade, bottle of water and so on.

I use the word 'lever' because these are primary tools that I strongly recommend you consider deploying first with your client before any others.

They can create maximum leverage for change and as a result will help win more desired outcomes long term. Leverage is a word that often worries some coaches and it shouldn't. It's the main scientific mechanism that early Eygptians used to build the pyramids. Getting someone to commit to a goal and/or themselves can be more challenging that you think requiring a lot of candour and significant leverage, but let's get clearer on these levers. If you could only have seven major coaching levers that are designed to leverage results quickly what would they be?

I love asking this question to a coach because their list will say so much about their style, passions, methodology and 'coaching DNA'.

I think I would be a little concerned if my chosen levers never appeared on the lists of other coaches though I have yet to meet any coach who has exactly the same seven as another coach. On the other hand, I do occasionally encounter someone whose only tool is a coaching model, and if this is you I would encourage you to have a look at the levers because they are easy to adopt and good for your client.

The 7 Guerrilla Levers then are outlined fully in Chapter 4. If you like what you see and are itching for further devices then take a stroll into the Coaching Vault, in Chapter 6.

Summarising the 'guerrilla' in Guerrilla Coaching

When looking at synonyms for the word 'guerrilla' the most appropriate matches include: *casual, irregular, unorthodox, resistant, flexible, determined, underground and 'David v Goliath'.*

Let's review the Big Picture.

- The Guerrilla Wheel provides a coaching 'map' identifying 7 Tumblers or keys to opening the 'safe' also known as the sub-conscious mind.
- The wheel includes 6 Interventions or areas of possible coaching focus. How many of these you would choose to use with a coachee is very much your decision and will of course depend on the situation.
- Underpinning these 6 Interventions are 5 Guerrilla Coaching Values – your coaching 'compass' and...
- Finally there are The 7 Guerrilla Levers which are specifically for leveraging the best results in the shortest period.

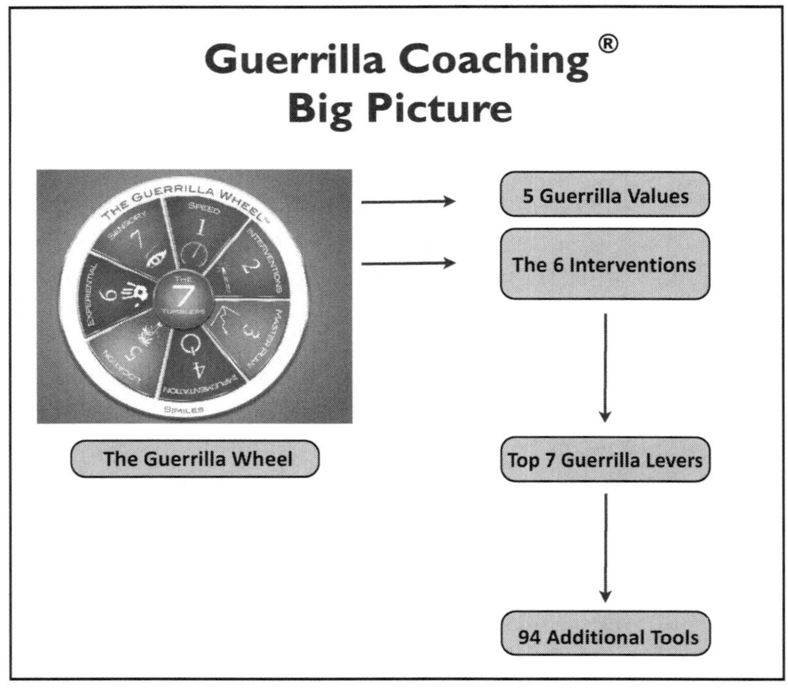

Now it's time to go even further down the rabbit hole.

3

RABBIT IN THE HEADLIGHTS

First Tumbler: Speed

Have you ever been caught in the headlights? A time when suddenly the spotlight turns on you and you have to respond immediately with all eyes and ears in your direction? It can be quite a startling experience and either you were able to come through with flying colours or you just froze and later on wished there was some way you could rewind time and be given a second chance.

All of us will have had this 'rabbit in the headlights' experience at some point, but have you ever thought of actually creating it on purpose with a client using it as a technique when they least expected it, in order to ask them some insightful questions and get some candid answers?

It's best done with full eye contact followed by complete silence after you've posed your question. Sounds daring, possibly alarming, but boy does it work. Provided you have created sufficient rapport with your client you have very little to lose and everthing to gain by turning on the headlights.

I normally do this using 'pattern interrupt'. As I'm chatting to the client, I suddenly ask them a poignant question they are least expecting by interrupting the pattern of their thinking. This method is the most likely to get me a true, completely unedited reply.

TV Detective Columbo uses pattern interrupt in every episode of the hit TV series *Columbo* that first aired in the 1970s. He would always use it on his top suspect who he believed to be the murderer. It invariably gave him insights he would never have gleaned from traditionally working up to the question and in effect warning the suspect that a tough question was on the way.

Just to give you a flavour, some of my favourite 'rabbit in the headlight' questions around goal achievement include:

1. *How serious are you about achieving your primary goal right now?*
2. *What score is the importance of its attainment on a scale of 1-10?*
3. *What's been your top excuse for not achieving it so far?*

I always get a much greater understanding on what's standing in their way of achieving the goal this way, not only by the content of the reply, but also the way they deliver it.

Take the word 'serious' in the first question. If a person says they are serious yet scores less than 10 then surely they're not serious at all.

Quite serious, reasonably serious and fairly serious which all attract lower scores aren't completely and utterly serious are they?

Here's another rabbit in the headlights question: "Does your behaviour match your goals?"

I really love asking this and observe a client's mental cogs spin into action as they realise the personal performance implication in the question. Painfully, I ask it of myself nearly every day. It's a tough one because there's always something more I could be doing. Or worse –

the realisation that I'm just not taking enough action directed towards my most important goals.

When clients say that their behaviours do match their goals then I challenge them some more and ask for tangible evidence which is more rabbit in the headlights methodology. Being more confronting, challenging and playing 'devil's advocate' quickens the coaching process no end and though it may go against the grain from a traditional perspective; politely asking for answers from your coachee in friendly smiley way versus using fast edgy questions, brings speed into the equation and a vital factor that I call a 'tumbler'. When you coach in a speedy fashion it enhances responses, increase awareness and insights whilst getting more adrenaline rushing around the systems of both coach and coachee. Bi-products are excitement, motivation and inspiration.

Another major benefit of spontaneously placing someone in the headlights is about giving them the courage to quickly self-evaluate their situation in a way they rarely ever do. This inevitably leads to a faster more intuitive decision being made even if there is pain attached. We all have wanted to run away from big decisions from time to time rather than have the courage and discipline to create a solution whilst looking directly toward the consequences that the decision may lead to.

The other element in the Speed Tumbler is time. If we lived forever we could put off all major decisions for a few hundred years. Wouldn't that be cool? The fact is, we we don't have that luxury. So introducing Speed as a prime coaching concept has two major advantages.

Firstly it creates more realistic appraisals for the benefit of coach and coachee. Someone being caught off guard can create more hand-on heart answers. Speed makes us more likely re-think on the spot and cajoles us into consider new alternatives.

Secondly it maximizes our most valuable limited resource called time. Expecting quicker responses from speedier questions stimulates the client's subconscious to appreciate that time is limited which it most certainly is.

The Time Chequebook

I tried an experiment at a corporate event and I went up to a member of the audience and I asked whether she had a £10 note on her. She paused before replying as she considered the implication of the question. Eventually she asked me why I wanted it and I quickly retorted with a broad smile that I was a bit short of cash and would like to borrow some money. With a nervous laugh she said she would not be able to help me on this occasion. I proceeded to tell the audience that I was doing research on how people react to certain questions. When the question had money at its heart, the responses nearly always indicated that money was something too valuable to risk losing.

Later in the afternoon I approached the same lady for the second time and on this occasion asked if she would mind sparing me ten minutes to help me set something up on the stage for the afternoon session. Without hesitation she nodded and asked me to 'lead the way'. I then smiled and asked her to just think about the difference between my former question about the £10 in the morning and my new question about ten minutes this afternoon. The first question was about borrowing money, something that I could physically return to her in the future, where the second question was about taking her time and, though she was willingly and prepared to give it to me, there would be no way of returning it to her afterwards. Suddenly the penny dropped and she realised what I was saying. I have done this many times since and the same outcome always occurs. I refer to it as 'The Time Cheque Book' concept.

Most of us have current accounts and in this day and age possibly even a cheque book knocking around somewhere. Yet it's only our financial cheque accounts that we appear to be aware of even though everyone also owns a 'time cheque account'.

Each and every day you are writing cheques from this account from a balance which continually depletes and will keep diminishing until eventually there's nothing left and the account gets closed permanently.

It's at this point you'll probably have a meeting with your time bank manager. I say this not in jest but in all seriousness because most of us have forgotten that our time bank and associated cheque account was opened for us at birth when a sum of time in years, months, weeks, days, hours, minutes and seconds was 'transferred' to us.

Unlike a money account we can't go to a hole in the wall or ring up a banking adviser to ascertain how much is left. However what's quite surprising is we are not prepared to give away our money yet very happy to fritter away our most valuable resource called time, to normally anyone who wants it.

Surely this is plain madness?

Time is our most precious treasure and unless we respect it and squeeze the juice out of it, we are completely blind to its true value.

It's when you link 'discipline versus regret' to the concept of the 'Time Chequebook' that you may start to fully realise the importance of this additional 'rabbit in the headlights' idea and why it's important as part of the Guerrilla Wheel.

For some rabbits that you catch in your car headlights at night, they will instantly take action and get out of the way to safety. Yet there are others who are frozen by fear and remain transfixed until they get run over. It doesn't matter who you are, where you are or what you're doing when the last grains of sand pass through the central neck of your personal hour glass, that's it, your time is up. You've caught the last bus home, the fat lady has sung her song and the party is over. As a guerrilla coach it's not my job to depress people but to instil strong enough feelings that will motivate a client to make important decisions and take quick action that could positively impact their lives forever.

Discipline versus Regret

Most of us have heard of the *Discipline versus Regret* concept. It's a classic coaching principle. When you want to achieve something of value, something that many people wish to also achieve, the chances are, discipline is the missing ingredient required to make it happen.

If discipline was easy rather than challenging, then everyone would put in lots of discipline towards all their goals and the majority of us would be attaining outstanding objectives as a matter of course.

In a guerilla coaching session, I like to explore the concept of discipline and look at what this mega-performance value would bring.

The way of making discipline more appealing is to compare it with regret. The moment you turn your back on the discipline of achieving something, you're shutting that door of possibility and opening a brand new one on the horizon called regret. Most clients get this quickly, and it's a big revelation. If the discipline can also become a habit, then true evolution or personal development becomes an exciting reality. Choosing discipline also provides a further tool to get things completed faster where Speed becomes the performer's number one ally.

Bringing time plus the concept of choosing discipline creates a powerful performance cocktail. It reminds me of when I was sitting in a café waiting for an old school friend to arrive when this very attractive lady started to approach my table. As I looked again I realised this was in fact my school friend! She looked amazing and nothing like she was at the school reunion nine months earlier. After greetings and pleasantries I had to ask her what had she done to look so good?

She smiled into her coffee as her eyes glanced up and savoured the moment that she would never have imagined nine months ago.

"Exercise."

"Exercise? You must be living at the gym!" I said thinking that I was also sounding quite rude.

"Not quite, but I have joined a gym. Correction, torture chamber."

Then my friend Ann proceeded to tell me all about Bodyzone situated just outside Birmingham where clients worked with a personal trainer twice a week.

"Why do you call it a torture chamber?"

"Because your personal trainer takes you to muscle failure in 15 minutes. And you cannot do another repetition of a particular exercise."

"And then what?"

"You go home. That's it."

I was amused and at the same time rather intrigued. How could you get any benefit in 15 minutes? It sounded impossible and yet I was seeing the tangibe results for myself.

"You mean to tell me you go to a gym twice a week for just 15 minutes a session and they take you to a physical state where you can hardly walk?"

Ann chuckled at this and continued to tell her story confirming that as tough and as challenging as it was, it was making a big difference.

At the time I was attending a well-known gym in Leamington Spa. Despite spending sometimes two or three hours there a week it seemed to be making little difference whatsoever, and what ran through my mind was: "Was this a good investment of my time?"

The resounding thought was for me to re-evaluate my exercise strategy even though the idea of getting more from less exercise didn't seem to make sense.

I ended up visiting Bodyzone and found that the people there were infinitely more passionate about helping their clients achieve their health objectives in tiny 15 minute 'time pockets'. So I agreed to start the following Tuesday when the trainer setting up my membership looked at me and asked: "Who will be bringing you?"

"Bringing me?"

"Yes we advise that someone drives you here because you may not be in a fit state to drive back."

After a brief pause he gave me a cheeky grin. Amused that he was pulling my leg I thought no more of it. When I in fact attended the session and got off the apparatus after my first rather challenging 15-minute workout, it suddenly dawned on me that I was having difficulty putting one foot in front of the other. I ended up having to walk around in a local park for an hour before the muscle pain wore off sufficiently to allow me to drive again and get home safely.

These guys weren't messing about they were very serious! I'd say a definite 10. I soon cancelled my traditional gym membership and ever since I have been attending Bodyzone. I use this story a lot with new clients because they are probably in a similar situation themselves about the coaching. How can you achieve much more in less time?

Less is very certainly more if you approach objectives with the right mindset and use appropriate techniques.

Is it a comfy ride over several hours that you want to give your client? Or a shorter sharper experience that may include temporary discomfort – like the kind you experience in the gym – yet leads to the creation of more challenging commitments that if adhered to means total success.

Speed Stuns

Another personal effectiveness tool around getting things done quickly that I've always enjoyed using is *Speed Stuns*. In business, particularly retail, if you're able to do something for a customer really fast, not only does it impress them but it impresses upon them the strong association of great customer care meaning they will want to come back to do business with you again. Equally Speed Stuns is something you may use on yourself. I'm sure this has happened to you many times in your life when you've taken on a task and rather than dawdle in your own sweet time, you decide to get it done really fast. Isn't it true that afterwards there was that feeling of euphoria probably supported by an adrenaline rush that made you feel good?

Getting clients to achieve things quickly is a worthy pursuit. We all invariably hate to wait for things and like rapid results. It makes us want to repeat the action too. Internet companies make a fortune on selling with speed to their customers and many are prepared to pay a lot more for a service that's a few nanoseconds faster. Speed excites. Speed motivates. Speed inspires.

More Speed considerations

Time and Timing

A true Guerrilla Coaching session should last between 30 and 45 minutes. If it's done over the telephone, we're talking 7 to 16 minutes. Guerrilla Coaching calls by telephone are best conducted early in the morning before business hours and some of my best Guerrilla Coaching face to face sessions have been scheduled between 7.00 and 9.00 am. Of course you can schedule coaching for any time but do remember that the later the time the more likely it is that the client's energy levels are dwindling.

The Fast Transfer of Concepts

Coachees get concepts more effectively if they are served up quickly rather than being explained slowly with too much detail. I love to carry video and audio clips and play them in a session. Another way is to have a portable white board or iPad and draw simple line diagrams to illustrate points fast. Of course there will be times when the coachee just doesn't get it and you may need to slow down or repeat something to ensure that they do, but getting more covered in less time does create a buzz and most people love it.

Quick Wins and Immediate Outcomes

A really excellent device is to give your client something to do within the next 24 hours and agree a follow-up conversation to confirm the achieved outcome. I've also asked a client to take action within the face-to-face session itself. For example, getting a sales person to make a call using tools you've coached them on, either in front of you or on their own, yet looking for a quick win within minutes.

As a Guerrilla Coach I would suggest that it's your role to get your client winning fast and frequently. This will boost their confidence in themselves and in you in a way that's rarely achieved at a snail's pace.

Client Alignment Check

In order to be clear about the use of speed when coaching, it's certainly not about speaking twice as fast or rushing your client into making decisions just for the sake of it. What speed is about, is coaching in small bite-size chunks within a relatively short time frame and choosing the quickest methods to get points across that encourage responses, interaction and shared responsibility working in a 50:50 partnership.

Inevitably there will be those clients who talk slowly and love lots of juicy detail. I recently had one such client who just loved taking time to communicate in the session and talking without allowing me to get a word in edgeways. I was able to deal with this by using a pattern interrupt then going back to our initial discussions about how guerrilla coaching worked. She had forgotten, apologised and we were back on a speedier track again.

It's important, prior to the first coaching session, for coach and coachee to be absolutely aligned to the rules they are jointly signing up to including understanding the importance of Speed.

Here are some of the other things you may wish to consider putting into a Client Agreement to ensure a fast pace is set and understood:

- Honesty and integrity at all times
- Open-mindedness on both sides
- A 50:50 working relationship with joint responsibility for outcomes
- Sticking to the time allocated for the session
- Being candid with each other
- Sticking to any commitments made on either side
- Taking personal responsibility for all things that belong to you (including communication)

This can be quite an extensive list and the above are merely suggestions. I would normally choose a minimum of three and a maximum of seven on a standard agreement

In summary, anyone can use the 'rabbit in the headlights' concept in coaching which is about spontaneity and speed through synergy.

Things often happen to us suddenly and we have to react quickly and positively rather than freeze with fear with potentially negative consequences. But we can also use this as a coaching tool to get a more insightful understanding of who our client is and what belief systems they are currently signed up to. 'Rabbit in the headlights' is also about the importance of time and how many clients don't appear to appreciate the true value of using it to maximum advantage.

Instilling a sense of speed helps people to realise that time is a hugely critical resource and if we get in the habit of doing things more quickly, we're tend to achieve a larger volume of results in our relatively short lifetimes.

Naturally there will be those who cite speed with making mistakes. Mistakes can be made at any Speed, and flipping it, sometimes there's potentially more to learn from making more mistakes.

Although Speed is not a traditional coaching concept, I can't recommend highly enough. But when will you next use it? How about right now? Provided it's a sociable time of day I challenge you to call a client and offer them an inspirational thought completely out of the blue. You may also choose a family member or friend and tell them how much you appreciate them. The call should only last 3 minutes and the objective is that they get a huge buzz from this fast paced yet highly genuine communication. Go on, defy the mental chatter. I dare you to do it now.

4

FUNDAMENTAL ACHIEVEMENT TOOLS

Second Tumbler: Interventions

In coaching individuals and groups over time I have defined 6 Interventions or target coaching areas that emerge time and time again. Here we explore what they are and the coaching devices that sit behind them. Though there are potentially hundreds of tools, we are going to home in on 7 Guerrilla Levers in particular. But first, let's remind ourselves of common challenges that coachees face that in turn create barriers to success.

1 – Change

Coaching is sometimes synonymous with change management. So much on personal development is linked to change and here is a quick reminder of some of the other associated words: *Transformation, metamorphosis, transition, conversion, adjustment, correction, diversification, modification, shift, switch, reversal, reclassification, remodel, refinement.*

Clients come to us for change solutions but is this what they really want?

Twenty years ago it was certainly the done thing to talk about change and how important it is: *change is the only constant in the universe you can rely on*. Yet as time marched on it became more curious that perhaps change may not be what coaching and personal development was about after all.

Just think about those people closest to you that have some really frustrating or annoying habits, and yes you've probably thought wouldn't it be fantastic if they could change. The only downside is that in completely changing their habits they may create a brand new persona and with this delete the things you've always loved about them. So in this scenario, would change be the thing you'd really want?

The word that makes much more sense instead of change is surely *evolution*. When you help people to evolve they're doing so from a start point of fundamentally being themselves yet transforming in ways that make them better off without necessarily losing their core identity.

So whenever asked by clients, "Will I have to change?" my response is: "No, I'd rather you don't. Continue to be who you are and instead consider evolving in a way that makes you more effective and successful."

As we know from Darwin, living creatures never changed, they've evolved. So what about deleting change management, cultural shifts, and people transformation for evolutionary management, cultural evolution, and evolving people?

2 – Beliefs, Filters and Paradigms

When you look at the word 'BELIEF' can you see what's at its centre? It's the word LIE.

Consider this for a moment, that at the centre of every belief potentially, could be a lie. It's often said that who we are is the sum total of our beliefs. As any coach knows, getting a handle on core beliefs is central to effective coaching. Though it's never up to the coach to tell people what they should believe in, I do like to hold up a mirror to my client in order they appreciate the full extent of their encoded beliefs and how these mental building blocks will impact the ultimate way they go about achieving goals and objectives. One of the dangers of beliefs that become unshakeable is they grow into ugly paradigms that are blueprints potentially affecting people in very significant ways.

An Experiment in Paradigms

Take a group of people and then ask them to look at some holiday snaps to decide where in the world they were taken. I've done this on many occasions and the shots are from my own holiday last year. What you would see I will describe as follows:

- A picture of an Italian-style coffee counter with some really amazing looking coffees
- A Victorian style built house with balustrades and a mini round-walled tower
- A lush green field with quaint rural wooden gates and fencing
- A 5-star hotel with marble floors, chandeliers and a grand piano in the reception
- A beautiful swimming pool surrounded by an array of sun loungers with plenty of white fluffy towels

All photos were taken at the same location by yours truly. Now use your imagination for the moment and looking at this list create some mental images of what these photographs would probably look like then I'd like you to come up with the first country or place you can think of...

This is an interesting challenge because to some extent the pictures could be from anywhere in the world. What's interesting is that the correct answer has never been given to me so far and I've probably asked over a thousand people to date.

Over to you – final answer?

Here are the top responses I've consistently received: *Austria, Canada, Germany, Scotland, Bavaria, Italy and California.*

The answer however is India. These pictures were all taken from a holiday in Southern India. This exercise is a great expedition into the power of paradigms. Most people, including British Indians who have yet to travel there, have a picture of what they think India is like. This will have been fed by news programmes, articles in magazines and stories in the press. As coaches we are painfully aware that the human mind is packed with paradigms. The big danger area in coaching is that there will always be a number of major paradigms in the mind of each potential coachee that leverage extreme acts of self-sabotage upon the individual that in turn curbs self-confidence and builds bulging barriers to their success. Starting each coaching session with a paradigm buster massively shifts your client's perspective on things and is a coaching tip I would highly recommend. You can find endless paradigm challenges on the net.

3 – The Interference Factor

Someone once said that personal effectiveness is *potential minus interference* and this is a really simple way of appreciating how significant the impact of interference is on the psychology of achievement.

Many describe interference as that little voice in one's head constantly chattering away. It's neither good nor bad for most of us, though for some it can be an incessant stream of devastating negativity.

A nice little coaching remedy that I learned from top business speaker Steve McDermott is the use of an elastic band to be worn on your wrist. Every time negative interference infects your thinking, twang the band. Psychologists have used this method for many years and it's surprisingly effective. The other way to deal with negative interference, is the reading of positive statements every day and we will be looking at these amazingly effective mindset techniques in due course.

4 – The Top 5 Success Barriers

- Low self esteem
- Displacement Activity
- Opportunity Blindness
- Lack of Goals
- Success Avoidance

There is a lot of truth in the concept that people are more afraid of succeeding than they are of failing. The people who are normally afraid of failing tend to be successful already. As strange as it sounds, though individuals say they want to succeed, it normally requires a major massive mental shift – and as most of us hate changing it tends to be an insurmountable wall for a good many.

The above list is probably much longer though it gives you an idea of some of the things that stop people getting what they dearly want. When you look at things like Opportunity Blindness, that's where coachees have switched off their brain's attention system on a particular objective and they are no longer able see possibility in life as it stands around them.

For example, if a client could not see a way they would be able to afford their dream home, even though opportunities presented themselves they would be oblivious to them.

Too many walk around without any goals at all so goal-lessness speaks for itself. When coaching teams in business and corporate groups, I have always seen an uplift in activity, sales and profits when each member of the group seriously defines and links their personal goal getting with business ones. There is nothing more motivating than a compelling driving goal, however tough it appears to be.

Then there's 'Displacement Activity'. A wonderful way in which to find alternative non important things to do in place of major strategic ones.

One of the reasons I spend so much time in Starbucks is not because I adore coffee or carrot cake, it's because being surrounded by so much chatter and activity makes me wholly focus on my laptop and complete the work I need minus the interference. If I were to sit at home or in an office working on my laptop I know there would be a number of displacement thoughts seducing me to think of alternative things I could do instead. Of course this philosophy for getting things done doesn't work for everyone and depends on the way your brain is wired.

Introducing 'The 6 Interventions'

There are a number of potential coaching scenarios that require a specific type of coaching application or *intervention* and I am aware of six in particular.

In any guerrilla coaching session consider kicking things off by identifying which of the six possible interventions would be most appropriate to use, coupled with choosing potential tools that sit under these six headings.

I use the term 'intervention' here to mean: *a coaching methodology for a particular target area that will potentially require focus and attention.*

A coaching lever or other tool will become the means to create the solution for this chosen area.

Why these six in particular?

Over numerous coaching sessions these are the 'six biggies' that clients have wanted most help in. When I think of an individual or business that I am currently working with I can easily attribute the coaching methods to one or more of these intervention areas.

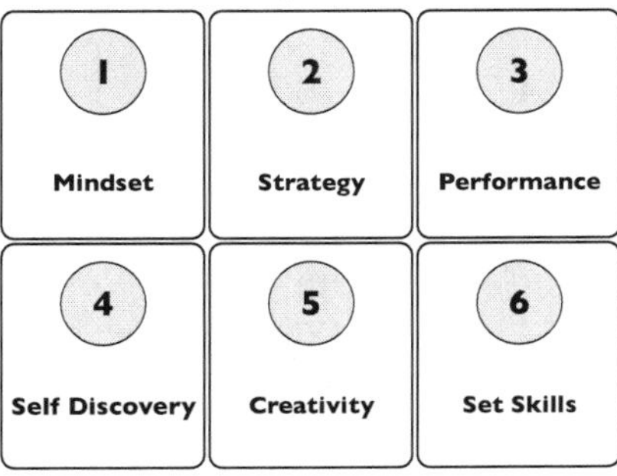

Intervention number 1 is *Mindset*.

Helping people evolve their often rather burdensome mindset is invariably the first major win. In a moment we'll explore the best tools to make this happen.

This is closely followed by the second intervention – *Strategy.* The difference between Strategy and Master Plan is that the former can vary from session to session depending where the client is on the journey whilst the Master Plan tends to be set in stone and amendments to this are usually very small. Each coaching session may not only require a different combination of the 6 Interventions but also a decision on the order in which they should be applied.

The third intervention is *Performance* and its importance normally comes before Self-Discovery because getting someone to improve their performance will create more self-confidence and a greater desire to discover more about themselves. Remember, though, nothing is set in stone.

The fourth intervention then is *Self Discovery*, and without this there will be little personal growth development. This intervention is also about ensuring the client is prepared to consider that they have infinitely more potential than they appreciate and it doesn't have to take a long time for one's inner 'genius' to become highly apparent.

The fifth intervention is often the most challenging one for most coachees, and it's *Creativity*.

My firm belief is that we are all creative yet few are prepared to acknowledge the fact. The reason for this is probably mental programming through our youth. We were probably complimented if we were seen to be good at subjects like maths, science or art, yet rarely were we told that we were also highly creative as a matter of course. The real reason for this is probably rather fundamental. Creativity wasn't a recognised subject in the school curriculum. There are normally only a handful of Creativity-related degree courses available at universities, and they tend to be linked to a specific discipline like art, music or writing. The message that goes out is that *people can't really learn creativity.*

I would suggest that no one needs to learn something they were already born with.

If you practise anything and apply it frequently, then your mind will open to it and you begin to evolve into naturally using whatever it is you are focusing on. This most certainly applies to creativity. Creativity is also a fantastic problem solver and therefore a key intervention area to target when coaching, provided it's appropriate to the goals and objectives.

The sixth intervention is *Set Skills* and relates to specific hard skills such as say – sales, marketing, leadership, customer care, personal effectiveness, communication, presenting and so on.

Choosing the Interventions

Let's look at a typical example of a guerrilla coaching session intervention selection based on a real client. Though I have his permission, I have changed his name. Ricky Thomas is a keynote speaker and is looking for some help to improve his confidence and at the same time discover some new ways in which he could win more opportunities for speaking engagements which would improve his income and have a tangible impact upon his overall success.

When you look at these six possible intervention areas for coaching here, which ones do you think are most relevant?

I could of course choose all six yet I want home in on three in the first session: *Mindset, Strategy and Performance*.

Once I have decided on the interventions I want to focus on I then explore coaching levers and techniques that support those interventions.

My final piece of preparation would be to create a 'coaching map' which is my final written plan for the session using a Tony Buzan style mind map.

The real benefit of thinking about what interventions are important for a particular session is that it ensures you never leave something really important out. For example, I've sat appraising coaches who at the end of the session have completely forgotten something critical like Mindset or Strategy. So the 6 Interventions is a great aide memoire for your session's infrastructure. Sometimes our excitement and passion for what we want to achieve can also create carelessness. And if we become careless we're not in control, and lack of control will create confusion that we pass on to our coachees who then are less likely to go on and attain amazing results.

Today with the world of iPads, 11-inch screen laptops and other mobile information devices all of these salient coaching reminders can be loaded, read and reviewed very easily in the five or ten minutes before the client arrives.

Desert Island Discs

Most of us will have heard Desert Island Discs on the radio and it's probably been on air for so long because it's such a simple yet wonderfully thought-provoking concept.

Let me now put you on a desert island as a coach and ask you to finalise on the handful of tools I asked you to consider earlier. Let's say you were limited to seven. Which ones would you pack in your suitcase?

Here's my list...

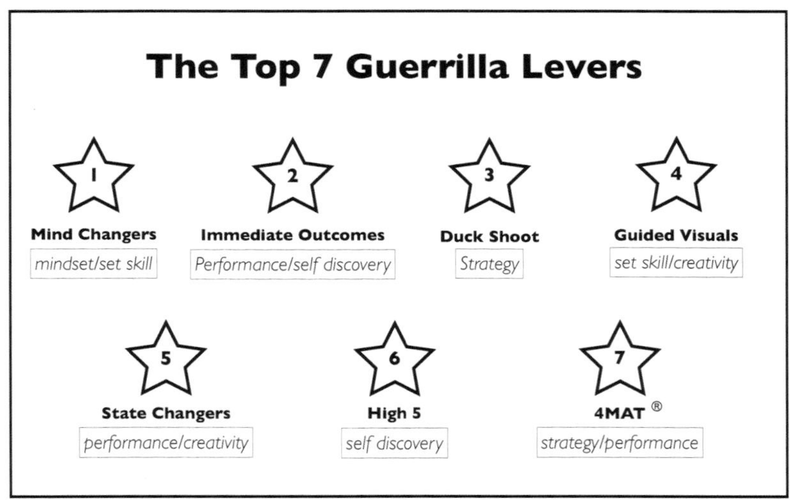

The '7 Guerrilla Levers' that underpin the Interventions

These levers are not being labelled 'guerrilla' exclusively because the majority I have discovered and collected over the years from various sources. The word *guerrilla* simply indicates that they would lend themselves to a speedy/focused/edgy/high-impact approach with any individual or team. If I was stuck on my desert island and still had to coach, I'd want to bank on tools that I knew will absolutely deliver the goods fast and effectively. If I was pushed to choose just one single tool, then I would have to choose it from this list:

Mind Changers
Immediate Outcomes
Duck shoot
Guided Visuals
State Changers
High 5
4 Mat

Lever No. 1: Mind Changers

Most of the Mind Changer techniques I discovered in 1986 from researching performance enhancers with sports coaches. A couple of them I had to adapt though all of them have been extensively used to create great outcomes by thousands of people I've coached since then. Full credit for success always must lie with the coachee because it's a simple matter to explain how the technique works; it's then up to the individual's self-belief, drive and total determination to convert the theory into tangible results.

I liken doing Mind Changers to doing physical exercise. It requires the discipline to take action on a regular basis and to allow the training (in this case mental training) to build and ultimately guarantee a successful outcome.

1.1 The Fast Forward Mind Changer

I remember watching a TV documentary where a top London football team sat in a meeting room around a table to discuss next Saturday's game. What was fascinating was to see that their conversation was being conducted in the past tense. They were talking about a future event as if it had already happened, and in this role play scenario they had already played the game and of course won.

The documentary then took you to the following Saturday and compared the original conversation with the results that transpired in the game. The next part made the hairs on the back of my neck stand on end. You would listen to the table-top discussion about who was going to pass to whom in order to score a goal and then flip immediately to the game for real and you would see the discussion being played out for real. They were making fantasy a reality bringing the future into now.

I'm aware that a few years after seeing that documentary, football coaching went through some sort of transition phase and there were even press articles mocking some of the more 'weird and wonderful' techniques being deployed in the game behind the scenes. Some managers then ditched using the ideas and went backwards in my view by using more traditional methods that centred more on practice and less on mental psychology. It was a big mistake and subsequently the poor results underlined the fact.

Rehearsing the future and the use of strong mental imagery through visualisation has been around for at least a hundred years and anyone in sports not using these astonishingly powerful mindset devices are playing with one hand tied behind their backs.

The best way to do Fast Forward is in a conversation with someone else. You decide how far in the future you wish to travel and then imagine you were meeting up at that point in time to discuss what had happened since.

In client sessions it's a great way to begin the session and immediately creates the right psychological environment for the rest of the time.

1.2: The Walking Fast Forward Mind Changer

This is a solo version of the technique and I encourage clients to use it daily. There is a lot of 'dead time' when people commute from place to place and this Mind Changer is particularly useful in these circumstances.

How it works is you agree a single sentence with your coachee that they repeat in their head as they're walking , preferably in time with what's being said.

For example, a senior manager who wanted to improve her self-confidence in presentations used: *"I'm amazed how my presentations now capture everyone's attention."*

For a whole month this lady repeated this sentence over and over again when walking from A to B and with no surprise to me yet by extraordinary coincidence to some, at the end of that month she was getting quite outstanding comments about her presentation skills from bosses and colleagues. Clients may also use Fast Forward when driving a car. They simply pretend they're using hands-free and chat away to themselves about something they want to happen – but always expressed as if it has already been achieved. Simple, unorthodox yet immensely powerful. We will look at it used in problem solving in a moment.

1.3: The Train

Many have traits and personal habits they'd love to remove or at least amend in some way and the Train Mind Changer is a great mechanism for achieving this. Here's how:

Imagine yourself sitting in a train carriage looking out of the window across to the platform opposite. There you see your twin standing looking at you. Suddenly you and your 'doppelganger' make eye contact and as you look at the person who is the spitting image of you, you also notice that they have all the traits or bad habits that you very much wish to eliminate. As the train slowly begins to move out of the station you notice how there's a feeling of relief that you are leaving your twin with those negative traits behind. In fact they are becoming smaller and smaller in size as the train picks up speed going in the opposite direction. As it's happening notice how there's a sense of joy, elation and relief as you mentally wave your twin goodbye. The very latest comment I've had about the use of the Train Mind Changer recently is: "Completely weird but it works."

The Pre-Shoot Routine

A similar mental rehearsal tool that basketball players have used is the Pre-Shoot Routine. This is where the player performs a sequence of events in their mind before handling the ball. In tennis Tim Henman is reputed to have used a pre-shoot routine before serving. He would do something like take three balls from a ball boy then bounce one back. It certainly made no sense to commentators who often remarked about the unusual practice he engaged in before commencing his service.

Sports psychologists would understand what he was doing. This form of mentally visualising the future in order that it happens for real is not just for sports stars – and that's the real excitement of understanding the power of Mind Changers.

Imagine having a 'pre-presentation' routine or a 'pre-assessment' routine for reviews or even a 'pre-closing' routine in selling.

Have you also seen tennis players in a competition like Wimbledon walking back to the baseline or sitting on the bench between sets and fiddle with the strings of their almost certainly brand new over-priced tennis racket? Now is this just a silly little habit that tennis players have in messing around with the perfectly aligned strings or is there more going on?

In speaking with tennis coaches I can tell you that very often some of the most unusual things that tennis players appear to do in front of TV cameras or crowds, is to set up a 'mental trigger' which automatically makes them fast forward their thinking in order to create a powerful mental image of what they want to happen for real.

Top players have these little idiosyncrasies going off just before they serve for example or when they need a powerful feeling to boost the belief in themselves.

This stimulates their subconscious to react in the way that delivers the most fantastic serve. Equally if you're watching top golf matches, you will probably notice how a player is about to putt and then suddenly stops and squats to look at the line of the ball. While you may wonder why they they can't just get on with it, what they're doing is not some mathematical calculation about ball trajectory but the simple act of seeing the ball go in the hole several times over, as a fast forward 'pre-strike' routine.

Seeing the ball go in the hole first is very different to striking the ball 'blind' and hoping for the best. The latter method is the stuff that frequently fills the heads of amateurs.

1.4: The Lift Mind Changer

The Lift Mind Changer originates from a famous study conducted at the University of Chicago reputedly in the 1950s when basketball players used visualisation and mental rehearsal in their pre-routines before actual games. The key experiment was with three basketball teams where team 1 was asked to go to the basketball court daily for an hour and practise throwing balls into the basket. Team 2 also spent a similar time every day at the basketball court, however they sat in chairs and simply imagined themselves putting the ball in the basket. For this team there was no physical practice allowed other than what they visualised in their minds. Team 3 was told to take a complete month off basketball practice and do nothing connected with basketball either mentally or physically.

After thirty days the three groups had their results compared. Starting with Team 3 who had taken the month off, their performance had deteriorated. Team 1 who practised in a purely physical way had improved their performance by 24%. However the biggest surprise was the result of Team 2 who had only used mental rehearsal and visualisation. They had improved by an amazing 23% which was a just one percent less than those who had practised for real.

Of course when athletes combined physical practice with mental rehearsal, their results became quite extraordinary. The great news is that coachees don't need to be a basketball players to achieve similar results in their own quests for greater performance and rapid success.

Instructions for the Lift Technique

- Sit somewhere quietly and close your eyes
- Imagine yourself walking down a corridor
- At the end is a lift or elevator
- The doors open and you step inside
- Turn and notice that you are on floor 18
- Now select B for Basement
- As the lift doors close and the lift starts to descend
- As the lift continues to descend imagine all the muscles in your body becoming completely relaxed.
- The lift continues to descend faster now

- 16...15...14...13...12.
- The further the lift descends the more relaxed you become
- 11...10...9...8.
- You're really enjoying the feeling complete relaxation
- You can sense the lift descending even further
- Not much further as the lift approaches ground level
- Finally the lift reaches the basement and the doors open.

Now imagine yourself walking out into the basement and ahead of you is a clock. Notice that the time of day is your favourite time of day and you have the option now to go to the left or the right of the clock. If you go to the left of the clock you're about to mentally rehearse something that you used to be really good at that you need to improve once more. If you go to the right of the clock you're about to mentally rehearse something completely new that you would like to excel in.

- There are doors on each side and you must decide now which door to go through.
- Let's imagine you choose the right door past the clock and in going through the door you enter a vast space. Here in this space you would rehearse whatever it is that you need to improve upon.

For example if it's presentation skills, you go through the door and find yourself on a stage in front of a massive audience who love you.

- You stay in this space and mentally rehearse for about two minutes.
- After this you return the way you came and come, past the clock which is now an hour further in time.
- This suggests to your subconscious that you've had much more mental rehearsal than the actual time you spent.
- Move back towards the lift, get in, select floor 18 as the doors close and the lift ascends.
- Now feel yourself ascending fast, going through all the floors from basement up to 18 again.
- As you sense the movement of the lift going up, be more aware

of your surroundings and your body once more.
- At floor 18 open your eyes in your own time.

The Lift Mind Changer is probably the most powerful technique of all. Well proven as a fantastic performance enhancer in sports, I always encourage coachees to adopt it early on as a daily mental rehearsal routine that opens up their minds to quite astonishing possibilities personal achievement.

1.5: The Flip Cards

If you've never used flip cards you're going to love this technique. You may use index cards from any stationers or those little cards attached to a ring and used for school revision. You need to create between 20 and 30. On each card you should write a goal, target or objective written in the past tense. Each card has a different goal though you may also have a number of cards all about the same goal. By all means add pictures and colour to your cards to make it more visually tantalising. Then flip through the cards once a day reading the past tense statement. You may even do this while you're on the phone because the most important mode of communication here is between you and your subconscious.

The Guy on Wall Street

In visiting the USA in the '80s I was given the business card of a top life underwriter who had an office just off Wall Street. He was a friend of a friend who was very much into personal development and when I arrived in New York I made a point of arranging an appointment to see him as I was given the impression that we could have a lot in common. As I walked into the reception of his well-appointed office I was greeted very warmly by a receptionist who presented me with this rather sumptuous menu of drinks and snacks. It felt as if I'd walked into a café attached to a boutique hotel. Ordering a rather exquisite sounding coffee, I also looked at the extensive array of quality magazines that decorated a small walnut coffee table next to an inviting black leather armchair.

Finally I was called into his office, and it was like walking into a luxury city apartment with views over the Hudson River. The room was minimal with an impressive glass table and comfy looking swivel chair. On the walls were original paintings and it didn't take much to work out that this life underwriter was a really successful man.

As I sat up at the table with my coffee the only thing that appeared out of place was a pile of index cards that seemed to take centre stage on the table's highly transparent surface. As he caught me glance at the cards he picked them up and started to shuffle through them.

"They're my goal cards," he said proudly.

This definitely had my full attention now as he explained his curious habit of writing down his goals, each one separately on a card and reading them at least once a day. It wasn't long before he allowed me to read some of them though I did wonder why he was writing down things he'd already achieved if they were 'goal' cards, given they'd all been written in the past tense rather than the present or future. For example one card said: *"I really love my Sunseeker yacht moored at Miami because it allows me to have fantastic weekends with my closest friends in the warm Florida sunshine."*

Here was a man who sold life insurance very successfully yet it hadn't started out that way. After many years struggling he had learned of this almost secret method of writing down what he wanted to achieve on a card in the past tense and then read it once a day.

Whenever you read anything in the past tense the subconscious will start to believe you have already achieved it and therefore when it realises that there is no tangible evidence of the goal, it does everything to get you to take the actions to allow the belief to match the perceived reality.

I've coached this flip card technique to hundreds, if not thousands of people over the years and those who have embraced the technique and passionately acted in making it a regular daily ritual have always reaped the rewards that inevitably followed.

1.6: The Star technique

Go buy yourself a set of stars or other sticky shape from a stationers and stick it on something that you see regularly. For example, your mobile phone, diary, computer, iPad, bathroom mirror, fridge etc.

Now take the same shape, ideally a star shape, (it reminds many people of doing well at school), and stick the item on something like a business card or plastic card and place it in your purse or wallet.

Once a day remove the card and look at the shape. As you do so make a strong mental picture of the next tangible result you're looking to achieve.

How this works is that whenever you subconsciously link the shape, you get a glimpse of your goal on items around you. This kind of reminder of what you are seeking stimulates the brain's attention system. The result is new awareness of opportunities that perhaps you would have missed without the technique.

1.7: The Image Diary

One of my favourite Mind Changers, the Image Diary is a scrapbook that contains pictures from magazines, newspapers and photographs of the things you want to achieve and realise in the future. You thumb through the pictures, preferably with headphones and your favourite music playing once or twice a week. This was how I originally coached the technique, though now with new technology I suggest having a PowerPoint presentation with accompanying music on one's laptop making this is an enriching and thoroughly enjoyable experience that works.

When you've achieved the picture you've been seeing regularly then you need to replace it with a new one. This also applies to the flip cards. Mind Changers are easy and quick to coach and clients can use them immediately. The key to ultimate success with Mind Changers is maintaining the discipline of daily use. I often challenge people to do them for 30 days and come back to me and tell me they didn't work. This particular challenge I've been issuing for over 12 years now, and hand on heart, not one person has ever come back to me and said it didn't work. I also need to add that a large number of people I've shared the idea with – usually people not paying me for coaching – never follow the advice properly and guess what – fail to achieve any results. Mind Changers will work, however, if you follow the instructions without deviation.

Lever No. 2: Immediate Outcomes

The first tumbler in *The Guerrilla Wheel* is that of Speed and as already mentioned, *speed stuns*. The Immediate Outcome tool then is about giving your client an immediate and significant experience that sometimes will take just a few seconds. The impact however is normally immense. Let's look at a few options:

2.1 The Ball Catch

When coaching a group I ask how many of them are poor in catching a ball, and there's invariably one person who puts their hand up rather sheepishly. I then invite them to rate their catching ability out of 10 and proceed to play catch with them in front of the audience. The more nervous they are and the more they feel they're under the spotlight the better.

I instruct all eyes in the room to look at this person so that the pressure on really on them and the first catch will very much match the low score they placed on themselves earlier. However, because I now engage in a conversation with them about something that has nothing to do with ball catching, within seconds, and often unbeknown to them, their catching improves quite dramatically. About thirty seconds later and after getting the person to catch just with one hand, I stop the entire experiment, look at the individual and ask them again how good they are at catching a ball? Invariably before they utter a word the audience have already decided for them that they are in fact a 10 out of 10.

I once had a man who scored himself 2 and realised he was a 10 within 11 seconds. (If you can get someone to time this it's a useful piece of hard evidence to give the candidate afterwards.) At the next break in this particular workshop he came up to me with a broad smile and once again asked me to explain how it had worked. The effect on him was quite dramatic and this *immediate outcome* not only made him re-assess his latent abilities but also who he was and where he was going in his life and career.

2.2: Holding your Breath

Get a stopwatch and time someone holding their breath. Tell them how long they achieved but also add a good 15 seconds to the amount. In other words lie to them! Now get them to repeat it but this time give them the stopwatch so they can watch the time pass in order to beat their believed score. I think you probably know what happens. They go for the score plus 15 seconds and beat it hands down. When they return the watch with a feeling of jubilation you then tell them how you lied to them about the original score and they usually stare with disbelief. This immediate outcome tool is definitely performance and self-discovery all wrapped up into one.

2.3 Arm Bending

When I first saw Graham Alexander do this in front of an audience in London it culminated in a few gasps in the room and I'm pretty sure one came from me. He selected someone who looked like they lived above a gym and invited them to come along and take his wrist and upper arm and make him bend it from an outstretched position. The first time it looked extremely painful as Graham gritted his teeth and used all his strength and energy to keep his arm straight.

Unfortunately we could all see that the gentleman leveraging the agony was getting the better of him as all of a sudden Graham's arm bent at the elbow and it was game over. The man was then asked to leave the room as Graham explained to the audience what he was going to do next. He revealed that when you make your arm muscles go rigid it makes it easier for the arm to bend in the middle. However if you were to relax your muscles without actually bending the arm and be confident in yourself, it would make it more difficult for the arm to bend. Finally the real magic came from imagining that you had an iron bar fitted through the entire bone structure of your arm and there would be no way the arm could be bent.

Just before I go onto the outcome of this story, do something very simple: put your arm out in front of you or to the side and I want you to imagine that at this moment in time you're having a completely painless operation where surgeons are pushing this rather heavy bar through your hand, through all the bones of your forearm and upper arm and now it's locked in place.

Okay if you're doing this with one arm in the air and the other arm holding this book, here's what I want to know: *does your arm feel heavier?*

So the volunteer comes back into the room and assumes the position in order to repeat the action but this time there's a completely different result. Graham is now completely relaxed and smiling and the so called strongman becomes the one who starts sweating and looking red-faced, unable to move Graham's arm at all. A complete reversal of the result. The *Immediate Outcome* is the realisation of the latent power we all possess yet are often totally unaware of and are clearly not using.

2.4 Memory Rooms

Before reading this section I'd like you to have a think about how good a memory you have. You may even like to give yourself a score out of 10.

Here's another *Immediate Outcome* you can achieve while you're reading the book:

- I'd like you to take a mental trip through your home and identify seven rooms or locations in exact sequence as you walk through them from one to the other.

For example you might have location one your front door, location two the hall, location three the living room, location four the dining room, location five the kitchen, location six the garden, location seven the garden shed.

Now be clear on your own seven locations in order.

- Okay have you got your list in your mind?
- If I were to test you now would you know the location and the number in the sequence?
- What's location three? What about location six? And finally what's location four?
- So far so good and I'd like you to go back to location one and imagine what it looks like in your head.
- Now in that location I'm going to give you an object to link with that location and the first object is a cup of tea.
- So for example imagine a massive cup of tea in that part of

your home and by all means you can be in the picture too and perhaps you're sitting in it.

- What's really important is that you make the picture silly, stupid or ridiculous in order that the final mental image is memorable.
- So let's move on to location two, think of your location and my word for you to link up with that location is 'Noah's Ark'.
- In the third location link up a maypole with streamers.
- In location four link up the word 'ray' which can be a man called Ray or the ray from a torch.
- In location five link up a policeman.
- In location six link it with a shark.
- In location seven your word to associate is a key.

So let's see how you've done. Please answer the questions below and make a note of how many you get right.

Memory Room Quiz:

1 What did you link with your third location?
2 What did you link with policeman?
3 What did you link with location seven?
4 What did you link with location two?
5 What did you link with the last location?
6 What did you link with the first location?
7 What did you link with a shark?

So how many did you get right? And has made you realise that you have an infinitely better memory that you thought? This is another example of an *Immediate Outcome* will demonstrate to your client that they have so much latent ability that they are probably failing to tap into.

The solution now would be to improve their performance with the right coaching.

2.5 Karate Style Board-Breaking

This is something not to try out unless supervised by someone who has some training in it. It's not dangerous when done properly, though it's useful to know the do's and don'ts and particularly the right wood to use which is soft pine.

With a volunteer who has a real desire and determination to break a piece of wood with their bare hand, it only takes a few minutes of tuition and encouragement to help anyone make a breakthrough.

Other pursuits include fire-walking and arrow breaking. These last two *Immediate Outcome* experiences definitely require people who know what they're doing and who have the necessary insurance as the former option is potentially hazardous when conducted by the inexperienced!

There are many other ways you can get people to experience that rush of self-discovery and improved performance in what appears to be a nano second. Professional magician and NLP guru John Vincent teaches a complete beginner how to present a visually stunning magic trick in a few short minutes with a mind-numbing outcome.

Also business entrepreneur Dean Thorpe has worked with snooker champion Shaun Murphy where it's possible to take a group of company employees and get them to perform amazing trick shots within minutes. You can imagine the euphoria that follows coupled with a sudden rush of self-confidence and a desire to achieve similar results in other areas of their lives and careers.

Lever No. 3: The Duck Shoot

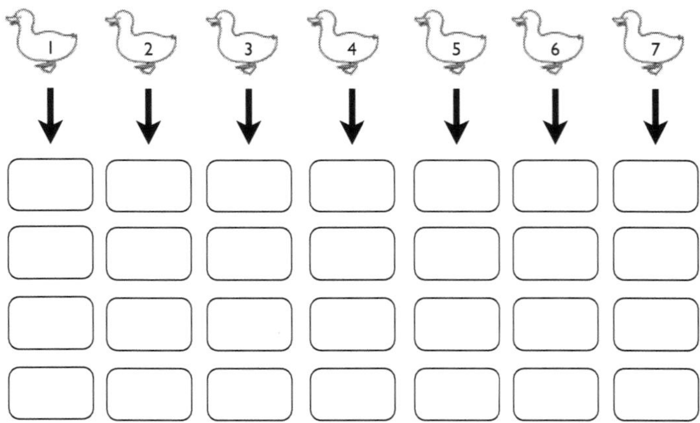

Business strategists and masters of business administration are prize assets to have as part of the team for any company that wants to succeed quickly. At the same time there's nothing like pure clarity of thought around a really simple future planning tool, hence presenting *The Duck Shoot.*

As you see from the diagram there are seven ducks and four actions under each one. Each duck represents an important goal that you need to achieve in the shortest possible time frame. You may consider having a duck shoot for your business or career and another one for your life as a whole. You should consider up to 7 areas of focus with a suggested minimum of 3.

So what are the seven goal areas you currently want to make headway in? Identify the subjects and enter this information on the top line.

In the four boxes under each goal list the four things that need to happen next in the chosen area and note that these are normally actions. When an action is successfully completed then replace it with another and then another, until the goal or goal area is achieved. Of course once you achieve this you can replace your duck with an alternative one. When coaching someone it's great to be able to look over their current Duck Shoot and the state of play with all focus areas. The alternative to a Duck Shoot would be something like a mind map, and I always suggest to clients that they avoid linear notes and old-fashioned business plan formats, though a set of financials attached is always highly recommended.

Lever No. 4: Guided Visuals

To undertake a Guided Visual you would probably need some privacy. The reason is that the individual needs to sit comfortably in a chair with their arms and legs unfolded and their eyes shut.

When doing this with a client I normally take them on an auditory journey and suggest visual images that would relate to their desired outcome.

This guided visual process could also be about skills, feelings or personality traits. It's a great way to complete a session, particularly when you include things from the coaching which you want them to be aware of and remember as they leave you.

What's even more powerful is the technique conducted with two or even three additional voices. The coachee should sit in a chair with their hands on their lap and their feet apart firmly on the floor. There would be one voice standing at the back of them, one voice nine inches from their left ear and the third voice nine inches from their right ear. Having established what the subject is for this guided visual, the three voices then speak in unison, in a very low volume so that the receiver gets all three inputs at the same time. For example if the subject is once again better presentation skills:

> VOICE ONE: You are standing in front of a large audience and notice how they're anticipating the start of your presentation.
>
> VOICE TWO: On this occasion you are feeling supremely confident and can't wait to impart the knowledge and ideas you've prepared as a treat for this group.
>
> VOICE THREE: Notice how everyone in the room is sitting at the edge of their seat waiting to hear what you have to say and taking lots of notes...

Providing the individual relaxes and sits back while letting it all happen, it is actually a very relaxing and enjoyable experience. (Try doing this with some friends of yours and request to be on a beach having a wonderful holiday!)

Although the conscious mind is unable to listen to all three conversations individually, the subconscious can do just that. It takes in all the information and processes it at the same time. A clever and very effective device.

Lever No. 5: State Changers

As Guerrilla Coaching is very much about speed, changing one's mental/physical state quickly is an important requirement in the process. In order to get someone to transform their state fast, conversation may well be a good starting place given that words are extremely powerful devices, and I place a lot of store on some fundamental NLP technology that I'm pretty sure most coaches are using or aware of these days. Nevertheless, in order not be too assumptive let's take a look at some of the well-known NLP tools which are ideal for the guerrilla approach.

5.1 The Swish Technique

The Swish Technique gets its name from the swishing sound you may use during the procedure. The purpose of the technique is to replace negative feelings with positive ones. Every time you use Swish you're creating a new direction in your thinking from negative to positive, going from not useful to resourceful.

Here are the instructions:

- Begin by creating the ideal feeling in a detached way, turn up the visual, auditory and feeling-based aspects to the image so it becomes compelling.
- Now see a large poster-size picture of the item or feeling you want to remove with a small postage-size version of the ideal item/feeling you want to create next to it.
- Here's where the swish comes in. Imagine the large image shrinks immediately and the the small image balloons to take it's place instantly with the 'swish' sound completely obliterating the original image which has shrunk and disappeared into obscurity. It all happens in a split second.
- After each swishing think of something else to clear your mind.
- Keep swishing for at least half a dozen times until you find it difficult to maintain the unwanted picture or feeling anymore.

In my experience not every technique will work on everyone. Yet I have always found there's always at least one that will work and work rather well.

5.2 Circle of Excellence

The Circle of Excellence should be practised in a place where there is plenty of room. The most successful examples of this are those with circles actually drawn on the floor or created with a carpet though the usual way is to have an imaginary circle of about one metre in diameter and certainly large enough to walk into. I would then get the coachee to imagine that inside the circle is all the feelings of their ideal state of being.

For example feeling full of confidence, energy and resourcefulness for someone with low self esteem. I've used this with a writer in order that she became more creative and confident in herself alongside her skills and abilities. The next part is where the magic happens. It's getting the person to step inside the circle and 'bathe' in the feelings just imagined.

A useful tip is to create an 'anchor' or trigger that they fire off when they step into the circle. This is something physical like snapping of their fingers or clapping of their hands etc. The other possibility is to have a smaller circle within the main one where you suggest the individual doubles up on the feelings and emotions by stepping into the smaller one.

Cynics often think that this is a lot of 'mumbo-jumbo', yet science will confirm that the brain can't tell the difference between what is imagined and what is real and when visualising and mentally rehearsing regularly.

It's actually about confusing your subconscious into accepting that the new preferred behaviour is quite acceptable as the norm from now on.

5.3 Anchors

An anchor is a trigger. These triggers are normally associated in a visual, auditory or feeling-based way once more. There are of course olfactory and gustatory anchors relating to smell and taste. Some olfactory anchors can take you back decades in time while visual anchors can instantly create negative or positive moods depending on how the anchor is used. A quick way to create an anchor for your client is to ask them to select a physical action, or audible sound – or both – and to link it to a desired feeling or state. Then fire off the physical/auditory trigger whenever they next require the desired state. This is a rapid State Changer.

By doing this regularly it's a bit like charging a battery and the more it's done the stronger the anchor becomes. The proactive way to install or create an anchor is to get the individual to start thinking of a time which reflected the state they want experience again and at the high point of imagining it, then fire off the physical anchor. After a pause or break getting the individual to think of something completely different, the process may then be repeated and this should be done a few times.

Other anchors include 'spacial anchors' where in a presentation you could have a certain spot on the stage that would anchor people to humour for example and yet another position where people would take what you're saying in a serious way that also creates a powerful impact.

As a guerrilla coach I use anchors from time to time where appropriate and have at least half a dozen that I will use to improve a client's feelings about something for example.

I must stress that this is no more manipulative than a basketball coach using a whistle, the clapping of her hands or the shouting of key words that trigger better performance responses in the players on the court.

5.4 The Spin Technique

Not all techniques work for everyone and I have to say that this one doesn't quite do it for me. On the flipside, there are numerous clients who have found this technique truly astounding.

Here's what you do:

1 Think about something that you have a bad feeling about that you'd like to change.
2 Identify where in your body that feeling resides (is it your head, throat, chest or stomach for example?)
3 With your hands, pull out that feeling and make it into a ball which you now suspend in the air in front of you, and like any ball notice that it's spinning.
4 Identify with your finger which way it's spinning.
5 With your finger, spin it the opposite way as fast as possible. Increase the speed.
6 You may now choose to put the ball back inside you or get rid of it by perhaps throwing or kicking it out of a door or a window.

7. You may enhance the technique by initially seeing the spinning ball in a colour you dislike and when you reverse the direction of the spin make it your favourite colour.

Now note how the feeling may have changed.

5.5 The Hara Technique

Hara originates from the Japanese martial art Aikido founded by Morihei Ueshiba. Aikido literally means 'way of harmony'. It differs from other martial arts because it's mostly about throwing and immobilisation as opposed to violent striking or punching. Many consider it to be the martial arts discipline with the highest ethics.

Instructions for the Hara Technique:

1. Decide what negative thoughts you'd like to change – to make you indifferent about them.
2. Identify the Hara point two inches below your navel. Stand upright, hands by your sides and feet apart.
3. Notice your negative thinking is in your head and now take it out of your head and focus the thoughts two inches below your naval instead at this the Hara point.
4. Imagine all your thinking now is focused at your navel like a laser beam and notice how much stronger you feel.
5. As you do this reflect once more around the negativity and ask yourself whether you feel exactly the same or does it feel better? Perhaps more of a feeling of indifference about the negative?

Hara is best applied to you by someone else taking you through it and the applications for this potent State Changer include: being more assertive, winning in discussions and the removal of negative feelings – even phobias.

Mind Changers, State Changers and creating Immediate Outcomes are once again all about speed. There are two more tools I really have to share with you, one of which I am confident many of you will already be using.

Lever No. 6: High 5 – The Problem-Solving Tool

High 5 is a great tool for self-discovery and may also be employed to deal with problems and challenges that confront someone.

If you imagine putting out your right hand and look at four fingers and a thumb. If your hand is placed palm away isn't it true that when challenged you tend to want to turn your hand around and push away that problem? The idea is to you have five options in the palm of your hand and there's no reason to turn your hand and push away the challenge and instead flip your palm towards you and look at your fingers and thumb and the 5 options you have available. The way to remember High 5 is that they rhyme.

- One is Done
- Two is View
- Three is Free
- Four is More
- Five is Live

One is Done

Now imagine choosing your thumb as option one and putting your thumb up to the world. So *one done* is a shorthand way of saying 'do it now'.

This is about the obvious yet most reluctant reaction to any negative problem.

"What action can I take immediately to deal with it?"

Very often when people take action on problems without delay they realise that the outcome achieved was infinitely easier than they were expecting. The opposite is also true that when you fail to take immediate action and bury your head in the sand, the thing that you don't wish to face gets bigger, more unwieldy and inevitably even more challenging.

Two is View– the future

So what is meant by 'view'? View relates to viewing the future and the way you can view the future is through a sports technique that has been around for over sixty years. It's extremely powerful and the great news is that it's very easy to implement, either solo or with others.

It's the use of *Fast Forward*, but this time for problem solving.

So here's a possible conversation one could have while driving a car as if you're on the phone. Let's assume the conversation is happening six months into the future about what's on your mind now: *".. and I think the thing that has surprised me the most is that six months ago I was wondering where on earth we were going to improve on our sales results and now I can't believe what we have recently achieved. I've just had a call from our biggest customer who's placed an order that has completely blown my mind! I can't wait to get the team together so we can fulfil the order and by the way it's completely turned my business month around because it was just so unexpected. I love this sort of thing happening to me and isn't it interesting how it's happening more frequently these days..."*

The reason Fast Forward is such an amazing challenge-buster is because when you are fast forwarding you often inevitably come up with ideas that you would never have thought about if you were not talking in the past tense. As extraordinary as this sounds it has been such a useful tool for *Immediate Outcomes*.

Fast Forward engages, energises and elegantly empowers people to be bolder, brasher and bigger with potential solutions and opportunistic answers to their perceived challenges at the time.

I once had an e-mail from the CEO of a well-known company who said that they were in a 'bit of a stew' and someone had remembered 'Two is View' in High 5. They broke for coffee and decided to do a fast forward over coffee. By the time they resumed there were 6 new ideas on the table and one of them was the solution they were desperate to find.

Three is Free– your mind

Freeing your mind is a most useful pre-requisite in any problem solving. There's a true story of a lift engineer who was working in a lift shaft on his own under the assumption that the lift had been switched off. Then to his absolute horror he heard the mechanism cut in and above him the heavy metal cage descending. He now had eleven seconds to do something before the lift crushed him completely. Stories like this one normally have a happy ending but unfortunately this one doesn't. What completely baffled his colleagues was why he didn't remember the most basic knowledge that all engineers have been drummed into them for this situation; that there was a way to reach up and switch off the device as it descended. Indeed, he had more experience than all of them put together. Yet in psychological terms, it's so easy to get locked into a 'mental blindness' when time is ticking away and you are 'naked' and vulnerable under the spotlight. If he could have in some way broken free from this fatal hypnotic spell, he would have been able to remember what to do from his training and save his life. Most of us know what we should be doing, and yet the 'busy-ness' of our lives very often locks us out from doing the right things that we only know too well.

When I first started coaching, the SMART formula was brought to my attention. It was interesting as a tool though did rather state the obvious.

Specific
Measurable
Achievable
Realistic
Time bound

Nothing wrong with this until I realised how boring it was. Who could get excited about achievable realistic goals? Here's another alternative:

Special
Massive
Amazing
Ridiculous
Today

Using NEW SMART in problem solving is much more exciting, I will engage these five factors with clients in asking for special, massive, amazing and *ridiculous* solutions whilst listing what they could do to resolve matters today.

It's also important to remind the client that the maxim 'things happen for a reason' is a concept worthy of attention when dealing with challenges. Some of the biggest ever challenges in your life may also have made you look more carefully at solutions, alternatives and opportunities.

So 'every cloud has a silver lining' is also relevant and true.

Also imagine a life without problems. Initially this sounds fantastic, yet if you were never challenged on anything, how boring a life would that not be?'

The 'R' Factor

In coaching a board of directors of a pharmaceutical company, they asked for critical assistance at a time when the UK arm was nothing but a fledgling business and very much about to fall off the tree.

I challenged the room to think of ridiculous solutions from NEW SMART, having exhausted all the sensible ones. This somewhat unorthodox approach saved the day, as one of the directors piped up with a most ridiculous solution. She suggested that they remove the sales team of over 300 people which cost the company a fortune in basic salaries and instead they sell everything online. There would have been laughter in the room if it had not been such a serious meeting and after ten whole seconds of complete silence there was a sudden ripple in the room that this completely and utterly ridiculous suggestion could have some merit. It was partly the answer as they downsided the sales team and sold much more on line, and years later the company are still trading. Admittedly this was a problem for some of their salespeople, though I imagine using High 5, it was an opportunity for them too...

Four is More– information

Tony Buzan's mind maps are a simple yet highly effective problem solving tool because of the way they take the mind down a mind-journey of discovery. A way that is not so easy to achieve without the visual structure a mind map provides.

The leverage is created by allowing your mind to wander down branches then twigs while you think through new 'solution avenues'. When a group is contributing to all the possibilities, it can really get

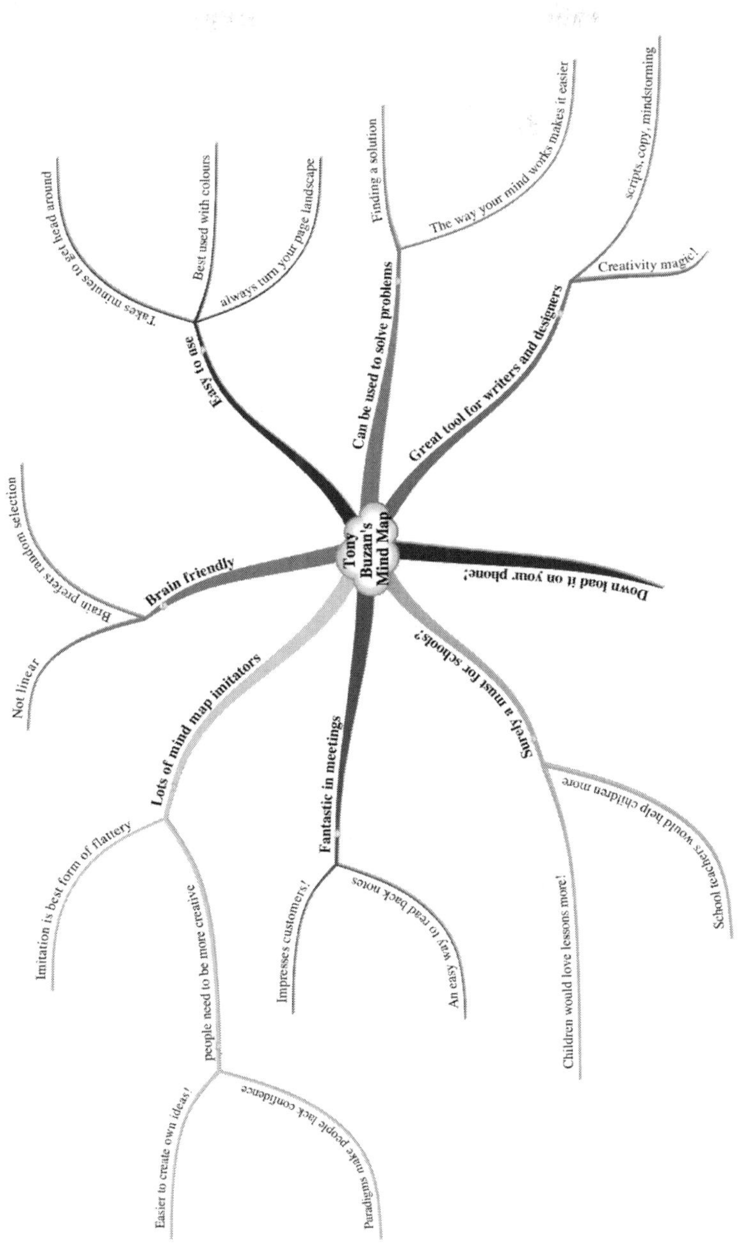
Tony Buzan's Mind Map
Easy to use
Takes minutes to get head around
Best used with colours
always turn your page landscape
Can be used to solve problems
Finding a solution
The way your mind works makes it easier
Great tool for writers and designers
Creativity magic!
scripts, copy, mindstorming
Down load it on your phone!
Surely a must for schools?
School teachers would help children more
Children would love lessons more!
Fantastic in meetings
Impresses customers!
An easy way to read back notes
Lots of mind map imitators
Imitation is best form of flattery
people need to be more creative
Easier to create own ideas!
Paradigms make people lack confidence
Brain friendly
Brain prefers random selection
Not linear

exciting as well as insightful. Also a mind-mapped solution looks easy to understand, appreciate and ready to action rather than wading through linear notes for the same information.

Five is Live– mindshare

The idea is a live 'mindshare' or brainstorm. The best way to do this to grab hold of a flip chart and a group of people who are going to help you. Get everyone in the group to spend five minutes on their own thinking of solutions solo. This means when they come to the plenary session everyone starts to contribute immediately getting the buzz of answers flying towards the flipchart.

Guerrilla Coaching is the combination of the right thinking plus the right tools. And the tools can be as unorthodox as you dare.

ABC Coach

When the problem is the need for coaching, try this:

A – action/attitude
B – buy-in
C – commitment

So here is a nifty way to get to the heart of things quickly. Great to coach others to use too.

It starts with identifying the action or attitude that the client needs some help with, getting their 'buy in' around what they are truly prepared to do and then confirming what their commitment is going to be as a result of the coaching conversation.

An easy to use and very powerful lever for instant use anytime, anywhere.

Lever No. 7: 4MAT®

4MAT has been largely used in education or instruction where four learning styles have been identified which allow learners to be engaged and orientated. It has been pioneered by Bernice McCarthy and David Kolb. The latter's ideas of experiential learning and learning styles lie at the root of 4MAT. Kolb, who is well respected in the field of learning, postulated that there were four different learning styles that collectively catered for all types of learning and people. When you present ideas using 4MAT there is a better connection and what is being presented tends to be accepted more readily with fewer questions. When 4MAT is used it overcomes style differences and cements that all-important buy-in for the message. Bernice McCarthy, who has also pioneered the 4MAT system, identified a theory based on brain dominance.

The four styles were as follows: Innovative learners, analytic learners, commonsense learners and dynamic learners.

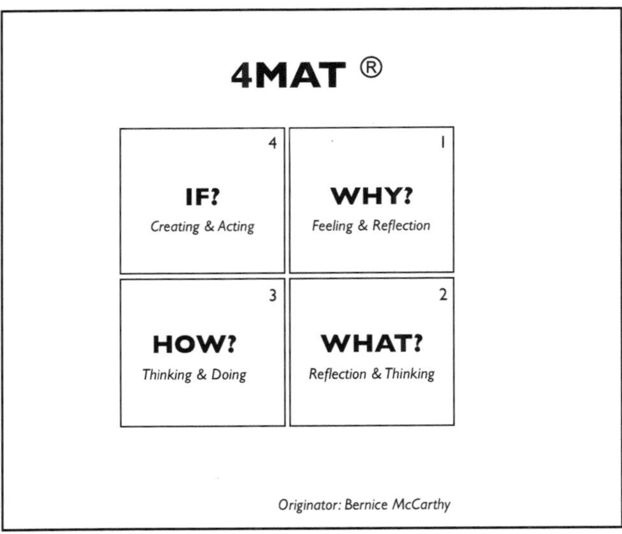

From these styles four questions readily emerge namely:

- Why do I need to know this? (Type 1)
- What is this all about? (Type 2)
- How can I use this to my advantage? (Type 3)
- What if possibilities? What might this create for me or others? (Type 4)

Now imagine using 4MAT for coaching:

- Why are working on this?
- What is the content of this coaching session and what must we achieve?

- How can I take away what I learn and apply it?
- If I make the coaching work, does this mean I can achieve even more?

It's also worth mentioning that 4MAT as a tool may be used really effectively for presentations and selling. It's that first question that salespeople often leave out altogether, the question 'why?'.

A couple of years ago when I was looking at changing my car I went into a BMW showroom and to my surprise and delight the first question the sales executive asked me was, "So Mr McCoy, why BMW?"

Needless to say, I now had to be extremely positive about the brand otherwise I would have looked really stupid coming into a showroom where I didn't rate the cars inside.

4 Hot Tips for Using Coaching Tools

If you've ever seen the TV show *Hustle* you maybe familiar with some of the special terminology used. I have adapted three of the terms in relation to how best to use a coaching tool that makes it much easier to understand and this has gone down so well in Coach the Coach workshops I have run in recent times.

Tip One

When using a good coaching tools always see if you can apply them in following three separate steps. I refer to: *The Hook, The Convincer*, and *The Clincher.*

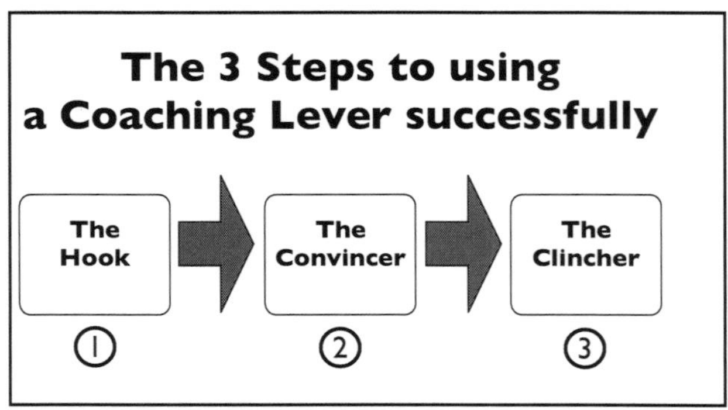

Let's imagine you want to coach 4MAT to a chief executive to allow her to be more effective in meetings and the presentations she runs. I would first of all think of a way to present 4MAT so it really gets her attention, *this is The Hook*. I might talk about the four learning styles of her team and ask whether she actually knows who is who. It's important when you're coaching to ensure your message attracts complete buy-in initially before going on to *The Convincer*.

With 4MAT, The Convincer would be to talk about the power of the question 'why?' then offer some examples of how it would enhance presentations and meetings with potential benefits that would emerge for her personally. I would in effect be convincing her.

Finally *The Clincher* is where I could possibly get the CEO to experience 4MAT for herself which could be in a role-play or getting her to use it in an upcoming presentation. We achieve The Clincher when in this case the CEO reports back saying that she's just used it and it works.

As a coach if you think about it all tools and techniques potentially have these three stages of development and the success will usually depend on going through the 3 stages in order.

I also use the steps when running workshops.

Tip Two: Creating Coaching Anchors

We've already explored anchors and how they work so it's time to suggest that you create a handful of anchors to use regularly when you guerrilla coach. Personally, I have three anchors that I use both in One-to-One and group situations. As I'm typing this manuscript I'm also smiling because I'm half tempted to tell you what they are and at the same time they would probably lose their power once people can spot them. I have had a couple of my colleagues in the past identify what they were which was really useful because I modified them and made them more subtle. Whatever you decide your anchors are to be, some of the reasons why they would be useful may include:

- wanting to get attention quickly
- desiring buy-in from your coachee
- wanting to create excitement or intrigue
- desiring to create inspiration or *immediate outcomes*.

Tip Three: The 1-10 Score

This is something that has served me well over the years and I assume that many coaches use something similar. Whenever I ask questions and get responses I like to take it a stage further and ask for a specific score out of 10. The challenge is getting people to properly identify what it is they're feeling or thinking. So if I say to someone how inspired are you feeling about this idea we're working on and they nod their head and confirm that they are inspired, is that inspiration at a 6 out of 10? An 8? Or an absolute 10?

It's like asking someone how serious they are about XY or Z and their response is a 9. To me 9 is not serious.

Whenever the score is under 10 the gap needs to be explored and therefore an opportunity to create a strategy in order to get the score as near to a 10 as possible, assuming that 10 is the desired outcome for client and coach. A great question would be: "So what has to happen for the score to be 10?"

I'm fully aware that a lot of people say that you cannot score 10 for everything as there is no such thing as perfection. I have to say, why not? If you can never score 10 for the things that are most important to you in life, I would regard this somewhat as defeatist. For those that say that by scoring 10 you can't go any further, I'd remind them that there's always 11, 12, 13 and so on.

5

SET-VET-GET

Third Tumbler – Master Plan

Why do people place so much emphasis on goal setting in personal development? Goal setting as such is potentially one of the greatest misnomers a coach can bestow on any client and I never have understood the way this concept is so mis-presented and mis-used.

Goal setting is also probably responsible for more people *not achieving their goals* than those attaining them effectively. There will be many who will wax lyrically about the importance of goal setting, but when these goal setters truly analyse how goals are realised, the goal setting part is just the front end of the technique.

I absolutely agree that very often the 'how' you achieve something will dawn on you once you are clear about the *why I am going for this* and the *what I am going for*. And in the absence of the how part occurring to you it's necessary to look at what actions are needed to *get the goal* without waiting too long.

Goal setting can also be problematic because our mind tends to take in information quite literally. Think about it. What does goal *setting* actually mean to a literal interpretative mental mechanism also known as the subconscious?

The answer surely is a shopping list. A way to potentially voice then park a dream with no indication that anything else needs to be done necessarily. And that's why people continue to set goals at the beginning of the year and reset them again the following year. Let's stop asking our clients to merely set goals and instead go all out in stressing the achievement of them with *speed* as an essential ingredient. The guerrilla approach is about starting the way you mean to go on and instead focus mainly on *goal getting*.

Semantics? Yes partly. But without abandoning the term 'set' completely use it as part of a triple action when you considering the achievement of goals as in: SET-VET-GET.

Decide on what you want, be sure you truly want it then create a robust plan to implement its attainment while allowing your mind to be open to further ideas and inspiration from your intuition.

So we need to move away from people believing that the act of setting goals is all the magic needed to be able to achieve them. We need to take the client further by stretching and taking the client to the 'edge' while aiming beyond.

Do you want to help people simply achieve specified objectives or do you prefer to stretch your client in a way that inspires and compels them to be addicted to go beyond their target and attain even dizzier heights?

That Well-known Harvard Business School Research Project on Goals

The most famous goals story may be read in Mark McCormack's book *What They Don't Teach You At Harvard Business School*. Here he cites a 1979 Harvard MBA programme study where students were asked, "Have you set clear written goals for your future and made plans to accomplish them?"

Apparently only 3% of the graduates had written goals, 13% had goals but they were not in writing and 84% had no specific goals at all.

The story goes that ten years later the members of the class were interviewed once more and the findings were that 13% of the class who had goals were earning on average twice as much as the 84% who had no goals at all. And as for the 3% who had clear written goals, they were apparently earning on average ten times as much as the 97% put together.

What's a little confusing is that in the early '80s I had already heard this story from a 1953 study at Yale University. The facts were exactly the same. Reluctantly I have to conclude that these stories are completely false and whoever invented the tale in the first place should be commended in attempting to inspire people to write down clear concise goals, which is good advice, but here again the focus is on setting not getting. It's also worth reminding clients that by focusing on the things you want rather than the things you don't want you are more likely to get the results you desire.

What's perhaps much more interesting is the whole philosophy about goal getting in the first place. Why should people get goals and go on to achieve them? It may also depend on what your view of life is. The school room concept is good food for thought. The idea that life is a school room and you're here to learn lessons. That in order to graduate you have to learn your lesson completely and you will be continually given the same lesson until such time as you do understand it. Surely one of the biggest lessons in life is about taking the initiative to be more proactive and grab life for all it's worth. It's like the stone versus the leaf in the stream. Imagine dropping a leaf in a stream and watching it go off in the direction of the current. However if you place a large stone in a stream instead it stands its ground and the water runs around it.

The question is: are you a leaf or a stone in the stream of your life? Do you go wherever life takes you or do you make a stand and decide where you want to be as life moves around to accommodate you? In coaching, inspiring clients to take a larger 'bite' of action will make a bigger difference naturally.

So when working with clients in guerrilla mode, do stretch, push and cajole them into going further by considering more detailed information at the outset. Some of the best movies ever made already existed before they were filmed because the director had a complete copy of the film in their head. To see it, hear it, feel it... and then step into the space of being it or having it Is what good movies and amazing goal getting is all about.

All of this will also constitute the need of a Master Plan and few people ever spend enough time in creating this 'tumbler' to open the 'safe'. A Master Plan differs from mere goal setting because it will have gone through a vetting process to ensure clear steps to achievement that have been worked out in detail. The first two interventions Mindset and Strategy are critical for the creation of any effective Master Plan.

In my twenties I was a paramedic with the London Ambulance Service and at the tail end of my time there, I decided to write a book on my experiences that was eventually published as 'Ambulance!' But it was a goal I had set without taking things much further. Then I realised I needed to take some more action but it all appeared so difficult.

After over a year trying to get it published unsuccessfully, I eventually decided to meet an early life coach in London though he described himself as a consultant. Perhaps I should say in retrospect that he was also an early guerrilla coach because he was very results focused and adpoted a 'no prisoners' approach. The reason I decided to take this step to meet him was because I had realised that I now badly wanted to get my book into print.

As I walked into his office near Wigmore Street, I sat down clutching my dog-eared manuscript. I was hoping he would help me find some magic way of getting my book published after all the time I'd wasted looking for a publisher which to date had got me nowhere. What was curious was his lack of interest in the manuscript and instead he placed all his attention on me and started to ask a number of poignant questions. The first one was rather strange and completely threw me: "When is your book coming out?"

I politely explained that the reason that I'd come to ask for help was that my book wasn't coming out and could he help? I once more reached for my manuscript but his body language soon made it clear that it was the last thing on his mind. He then repeated the same question to which I offered a similar response. Finally he looked me directly and explained: "Unless you have a good answer for me, I really do think we are both wasting our time. So, when is your book coming out?"

Suddenly the penny dropped and I realised what he was inferring. This was surely one of these 'positive thinking' questions so I decided to play along with him.

"OK, so my book is coming out ten months from now." "What day of the week?" Initially fazed by this really weird question, I muttered "Saturday".

"Where will you first see it, in which book store?"

"WH Smith."

"Which WH Smith?"

"Brent Cross Shopping Centre."

Then he asked me a really fantastic question, something I'd never considered before: "Describe the jacket." Completely put on the spot I started to spontaneously create an image of what the jacket of the book looked like in my imagination.

"It's a black cover with a strong image on the front. It's a picture of an emergency ambulance crew at the scene of a road traffic accident. A woman has had an accident and is in the road with her shopping all around her and the crew are working on her putting up a drip..."

For the first time I could see he'd broken into a smile as he sat back in his chair and I paused as I considered what I had come out with. When cornered I had become rather creative and I was then promptly reminded that the same creativity and open-mindedness would take me from no publisher to a publisher very soon provided I was serious.

I was also given some homework for the next thirty days to create a strong mental picture of the front cover of my book that I had clearly described and to see it regularly in my mind's eye at Brent Cross Shopping Centre north London on a Saturday, publicly for sale.

In sharing this story with a cynical friend a couple of days later, she asked me if I was really going to do my 'homework'. By then the whole idea had lost its initial impact and I smiled to her in a coffee-cup conversation and said that it was all rather silly and quite frankly a bit of a waste of time. Then I got his invoice. The agreement was that provided I followed through I would need to settle my account with him, though if it didn't work in any way he would credit me with his time and that would be the end of the matter. Of course in order to prove that it was a waste of time I had to follow through on the homework and it was this catch-22 situation that actually got me to take action.

In an extraordinary coincidence eight days later I was having dinner with a distant relation and I suddenly asked him a question that seemed to come from nowhere:

"Do you know any publishers?"

"As a matter of fact I do. Why do you ask?"

After a brief explanation about my book, he told me about the one and only publisher that he knew and agreed to connect me with her. In an extraordinary chain of events she was soon reading my manuscript, telling me that it would never succeed as a novel and was asking whether I'd be prepared to rewrite the whole thing as a piece of non-fiction. Though this was a bit of a blow, I agreed and soon received a contract together with an advance for £500 that was a lot of money then.

Within a year the book was to be published and the same cynical friend I had originally shared my coaching story with rang me up with much surprise to say she'd seen my book as I described in a bookstore that very morning. This was a surprise since I had not received my author's copies yet and she confirmed it was indeed in WH Smith at Brent Cross that she'd spotted it.

Quite excited I jumped into my car and drove to the shopping complex and in doing so I realised it was Saturday morning. Yet walking through the main doors of the store on the first floor, I wondered if she'd been pulling my leg because I couldn't see the book anywhere.

Eventually I located approximately eight hardback copies on a low shelf behind a column that was not where I had imagined I'd see my book for the first time. I'm not sure what possessed me, but I then decided to move my books, copy by copy, to a different place and a different shelf. OK, perhaps I did go a little too far and squeezed them in between two rows of books by well-known authors on the bestsellers shelf. (Why doesn't every author do this?)

Stepping back I then saw the original picture that I described in the office of the life coach in London, as my blood ran cold. Though I did the last part manually, the entire process started with a single thought that I repeated many times over and built on over 12 months with a plan of what I must do each day. This is what goal getting is really about. A three-part process:

1. Deciding on the goal, then...
2. Really thinking about it and deciding whether it was for me by mentally stepping into it. Finally...
3. There was the getting of the goal through a 'Master Plan' which was equally as important as the other two steps. Over the years I've insisted that all my clients SET-VET-GET when discussing how to get what they want.

The 'SET' in SET-VET-GET

1 Define your outcome vividly

When I ask a client to describe what they want, it's less of a conversation more of an interrogation, albeit in a positive way. I need to seek the details from them whilst also ensuring that the client is not talking about something that they'd quite like rather than this is something that they are totally smitten about and are prepared to do everything to achieve. What they put into words must above all be compelling. Also I would expect the client to step into their goal. See it, hear it, feel it and be it.

2 Define a Pin Sharp Image

The client also has to be pin-sharp in their description of the image they see in their head. If there is no picture there is no goal and it's likely to be merely a whim or something they've put on their new year 'shopping list' many years ago.

3 Sell it to Me

Once the client is in 'the goal-setting zone' it is vital they now take the reins and come back to me with a crystal clear description and story that engages me completely and captures my belief utterly. In short they need to convince me of what they want and in doing so they end up confirming and convincing themselves.

4 **Devil's Advocate**
Now it's my turn to see how strong a goal the client has created. Turning devil's advocate I will see if I can punch holes in what they've set out to attain and in doing this I will also test their resolve and true commitment.

5 **Draft a Statement of Intent**
In doing this I'm getting the client to sign, seal and therefore get set to deliver the outcome. In terms of the carrot or stick that should be linked to the goal, I normally choose both. There's a psychological understanding that most people are more likely to respond to 'away from' motivation as opposed to 'towards' motivation, but why take the risk? So there should be elements of both in any Goal Achievement Contract.

When Carrots help

I always remember the coaching session I had with a young businessman who was going through a rough patch in his newly-formed enterprise. The 'toward motivation' or carrot we put in place was an agreement that provided he hit his financial targets by the end of the year he would book a flight to New York on Concorde in order that he could get a haircut! Yes, he was going to New York supersonic to get his hair cut (at the place where John Lennon used to go) and this extraordinary 'carrot' was to be his reward for achieving financial greatness in his business. It also worked because the carrot was so out of the ordinary.

More Goal-Getting Tools

- **First draft, second draft**
  Rather like a scriptwriter writing a screenplay, your goals should go through a first and second draft process. This rarely ever happens in traditional goal-setting practices. Normally people write their list of goals and it's pretty much the final draft. It's about brainstorming as many possibilities as you dare in your first draft and then using the vetting process to take that list and chunk it down to a smaller number of targets and finalising your goals in

a final draft of truly desirable outcomes. When you get to the final draft stage you have both set and vetted which puts you in the best possible position to act on the getting of the goals.

- **Pushing the Boundaries**

  Why would a coach and coachee meet to evaluate goals if the coachee is not prepared to allow the coach to stretch their boundaries and take them to the Edge?

  Equally, why would a coach sit with a coachee and passively make a list of their goals, asking the odd question as opposed to playing devil's advocate to see what 'metal' these goals are made of? This is a classic procedure between barrister and their client accused of some horrendous crime. The barrister will take the devil's advocate position and poke/probe/challenge the client to see if their story is based on stone or sand. This is another useful tool for vetting the goal.

- **The Quad Chart and Post-its**

  Get an A0 sheet of paper and fix it to a wall. Now draw a line down the centre and a line the other way through its centre so you have four quadrants.

  Give your client a post-it pad and felt pen and then invite them to put a potential goal on each post-it. These goals should be short-term, medium-term and long- term as well as small, medium and massive. Normally I'd leave them to it and return after a pre-agreed time. Then ask the client to place the post-its in one of four quads. These are:

  1) Top left = would be nice to achieve
  2) Bottom left = ideally would like to achieve this
  3) Bottom right = very valuable/would like to achieve this
  4) Top right = absolutely essential/must happen

Part of the benefit of using this system is watching your client deciding in which quad to place which post-it note. When they've done then you will have the first draft and the opportunity to create a second draft with your client.

Here's both the SET and VET in one. The guerrilla approach would be challenging all goals that are not placed in the top right position.

- **The Warehouse White Wall**
  This doesn't actually have to be a warehouse; it could be any building, though there was one very memorable piece of coaching I delivered in a warehouse which somewhat reminded me of the set for Dragon's Den.

  In having access to this disused space and with the use of a ladder, some white, red and green paint with assorted brushes, the wall became the canvas for a goal-getting session – the like few clients ever experience in traditional coaching. The cynics would say that you could achieve the same thing on a sheet of paper without the mess! However, as I've discovered time and time again, there is more coaching magic using an unusual location, getting people to be more experiential and sensory about what they want, and the sheer spectacle of something that will stay in their memory, making it much more significant and indelible within their subconscious.

  In this example, we ended up creating a massive mind map yet also used large-size post-its and even A4 diagrams and pictures that had been printed off in advance. With a coffee percolator in one corner the experience became intensely exciting. I did have the sneaky thought of renting this space on a regular basis but then when you do something spectacular too often it will lose its appeal.

The Restaurant in the Spare Bedroom

It was 1987 and Ben and Maxine were in their early thirties and stepped into my office when I was based in Mill Hill, North London. They were amiable souls who always gave off large waves of energy and enthusiasm when talking about their projects and future aspirations. This was their third coaching session where they had been primed to come and sell me their dream. Ben pulled out a presentation that had been mounted on a large flipchart-size card. Clearly they had both spent a lot of time putting this altogether and I was pleased with them because I knew they were taking this entirely seriously. Their pitch lasted about 15 minutes and I was taken through their idea for the creation of a high-class restaurant for members only that they wished to create in a fashionable part of West London.

In terms of SET-VET-GET the SET part was very apparent, as I was in no doubt what they wanted to achieve and impressively the GET part was also in place because in their Master Plan they had created a step-by-step action plan complete with all financials. All of this did happen a number of years ago but even then the capital required to pull this off was £75,000. They assured me that they could raise the money from savings and re-mortgaging. Maxine smiled at me at this point and asked the inevitable question: "So what do you think?"

Well here is partly what they were paying me for, I mentally put my VET hat on. Whenever I go into VET mode there is an uncomfortable feeling in my stomach because some of the things I have to do, ask and say can come across as quite challenging.

If the party that seeks to achieve the goal is passionate about what they want one hundred percent and have done their homework, they should be able to easily deal with any vetting that comes their way, and as I duly vetted their business dream of a lifetime, I intuitively felt a little uneasy about some of their responses. I therefore made a suggestion that then was unheard of, though curiously I've seen a version of this idea on a TV programme recently.

My suggestion was that they set up this restaurant in miniature in a room in their home. The spend required to set up this mini model of the restaurant would be negligible compared with the outlay they would have to part with for their full-blown project. There would be only one table available and I suggested they should only open on a Friday and Saturday evening strictly on an advance booking basis.

After initial scepticism they got excited about this trial run idea and even suggested a name for the place which they wanted to call 'Illicit Encounters'. Tongue in cheek, they were going to tell all their friends about how they were able to offer an exclusive table in their restaurant that was so private if you were dining with someone you shouldn't be, no one would ever know! The other great benefit, was since they could only serve two tables a week, they would soon get booked up months in advance!

Though I communicated with them by telephone on and off during this trial phase, we agreed to meet for another coaching session after six weeks. This time when they came in I immediately felt a lack of energy and enthusiasm, in fact they didn't look their usual bright-button selves.

"So how's the restaurant business?" I ventured.

"The restaurant's closed," said Maxine with a sorry smile.

"What happened?"

"We've realised we don't like the restaurant business," bleated Ben who also looked a little embarrassed.

It seems that when they actually got into the swing of what this business was truly all about, they realised how hard work it was going to be and how they were committing not to two days a week but potentially seven. Yet by test driving their dream, the reality of what their desire consisted of hit home and had to be a good thing long term.

The good news was they were still £75,000 the richer with the option of re-setting their dream scanner for something that they did want.

No one can achieve a goal unless they commit to setting it in stone. No one can achieve a goal unless they have created action steps and a Master Plan which has been clearly thought through and no one should ever aim for a goal unless that goal has been properly vetted.

SET-VET-GET. Simple and highly effective.

So what about more on the 'GET' part? The next chapter will help here...

6

THE COACHING VAULT

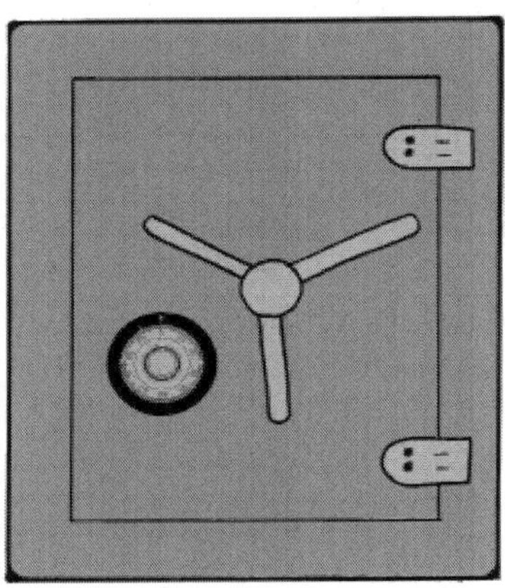

Fourth Tumbler – Implementation

If coaching interventions define the possible coaching terrain, then implementation toward goal achievement comes in the form of a veritible stack of coaching tools.

Welcome to The Coaching Vault and some further examples of coaching devices across the six interventions which are: Mindset, Strategy, Performance, Self-Discovery, Creativity and Set Skills.

I have chosen a small selection of tools in each category to give you a 'feel' for what I believe constitutes a typical intervention tool and how such devices underpin and create further leverage to enhance performance and success. In SET VET GET, this is the 'GET' part with the tools to achieve almost anything.

Though there are a limited number tools here, I have identified 101 in total and committed all of them to index cards. This way I can shuffle through them if I'm looking for something specific for a coaching session, and suggest you do something similar with your own favoured coaching tools. I also allotted each intervention groups with their own colour code so it's an easy process to pick up a set of green cards for example that indicate Strategy tools.

I would then choose the ones I want to use accordingly. Please note that each tool is referred to here with the minimum of explanation in order to cover more of them in my notebook style book.

Yet each tool could be used for a big part of a coaching session if the tool was appropriate for such use. As a coach it's a good idea to be aware of what devices and mechanisms you have captured somewhere and have available to you. Sometimes if it's a tool you haven't used for a while and it's only committed to memory you might lose it forever. You will probably not be surprised to know that I'm always on the look out for new devices because I want the very best tools for my clients. There is an old adage "It's a poor workman who blames his tools." My response to this is: *The workman and tool kit are of equal importance.*

Mindset Tools

1. The Four Breakthrough Principles

When investigating breaking a piece of wood with one's bare hand from a standing start as an Immediate Outcome tool, I asked a friend of mine who had attained a black belt in karate, to give me some simple karate-based tips.

I could then use these ideas to coach others around breaking a piece of karate wood for the first time in a few minutes.

The four concepts he identified I soon appreciated would not only allow me to break a piece of wood with my bare hand but also create significant breakthroughs in business and life itself...so here they are:

- Visualise the outcome you desire
- Aim beyond the target (wood)
- Do it with speed
- Have a reason why you're doing it

Visualise the Outcome

In any task you undertake seeing the end product means you're halfway there already. When I discussed writing this book with my publisher, one of the first things I wanted to do was to get the jacket completed. This is also where the 'Law of Attraction' comes into play. What the mind perceives the heart then can go on to achieve.

Aim beyond the target

A fundamental stretch principle of goal getting is to not just to achieve the objective but excel and over-achieve which creates the momentum to get exceptional results. However whether it be karate or another type of business breakthrough, if a client aims much higher, the essential goal is always likely be achieved. In karate style board-breaking sessions one of the reasons people fail to break the wood is because they're aiming for the wood and not beyond it. Sometimes I can actually see their hand slowing down as they come to strike the wood and that would be decreasing your speed as you come to the chequered flag at the finishing line.

Do it with speed

We've already discussed the importance of speed and how it can enhance coaching. There is also a confidence factor about speed because if you're about to break a piece of wood doing it slowly it must indicate a lack of confidence in yourself or just plain fear. In order to create a breakthrough, speed creates excitement, inspiration, momentum and a build-up that propels you to the top of the mountain.

Have a reason why you're doing it

The fourth top challenge in a board-breaking session is when people are slapping pieces of timber just because everyone else has been invited to. There is immense power in having purpose that you've properly identified linked to the things you want to achieve. When a board-breaking candidate is simply not making the breakthrough, I will spend just a few moments asking them to link the action to someone or something they feel passionate about. Once they get the idea they will go into that zone to the point where nothing will stop them making the breakthrough.

2. Sausages

Though I love to play sport, I rarely like to watch it unless it's something like a top football or tennis match. If we take football as an example, particularly World Cup matches, historically there have been those nail-biting penalty shoot-outs where unfortunately the England team have come unstuck on more than one occasion. Some of the worst moments on record have been against the German side. If you are a football fan you probably now know where this is going. Why are the Germans better at penalty shoot-outs than our own players?

From my sports coach connections I have it on good authority that the answer lies in *sausages*.

When I played football at school I always remember my games teacher shouting: "McCoy, keep your eye on the ball!"

In retrospect I now know that was really bad advice. Sorry Mr Thomas. When you over focus on something it isn't a good strategy and the eventual outcome comes into question. Apparently when the Germans take a penalty, they're coached to think of something else as they kick the ball. Imagine you're under the spotlight ready to take a penalty shot and millions of people are watching you.

Soon you're focusing on the ball and thinking of things like what if I miss it?

This is how our players appeared to be thinking in previous world cup matches where we lost in the penalty shoot out. Compare this with a German player under the same spotlight, running straight for the ball, fully aware of it and yet thinking of *sausages*. (The coach who told me the story may have been embellishing it slightly so I cannot confirm that sausages is in fact the image that Germans players thought about, but I'm sure you get the point.)

This is also how the *Immediate Outcome* lever using the ball-catching works. How you would use this in coaching, is to distract your coachee's attention when they over-focus on the thing they fear or have failed to achieve previously. This can be done by setting up anchors for them or in the case of a CEO who had a fear of public speaking, the creation of a sequence of things he needed to check off in the first two or three minutes of his public address.

When you over focus on something, particularly something

really important, there is a tendency to allow 'interference' into that thinking process which is likely to sabotage the outcome.

3. The Reframe

If you are unaware of this device then I'll explain its importance and purpose but if you are aware of it I wonder if you use the word 'reframe' when you're about to reframe?

A hot tip in reframing someone's thinking is to avoid using the word when you do it. By drawing attention to what you're about to do, you may also possibly undervalue the technique while reducing the other person's buy-in.

Most people are not too happy having things done to them.

The reframe is a change of perspective or altering the frame of an experience and if the coachee does it without realizing, it has infinitely greater impact.

One of the most famous reframes was during the 1984 campaign when Ronald Reagan's age was under the scrutiny of the media. In a presidential debate with Walter Mondale, Reagan nipped the age issue in the bud by saying, "I will not make age an issue of this campaign. I'm not going to exploit, for political purposes, my opponent's youth and inexperience."

It was fair to say that Reagan's age was no longer an issue for the rest of his campaign. It's often about taking something negative and changing the frame of reference to make it a positive. Would the impact have been the same if Regan suggested doing a reframe? So the best way to use reframing is just do it.

4. The 9 Dots

Many people today still like to use that somewhat cheesy phrase 'think outside the box', yet have absolutely no idea what they are saying or where the phrase originates. If you do know its origin it will help you to understand and think more effectively about what it really implies.

The way I use this tool is to ask someone to join all 9 dots in a 3x3 grid (as set out below) with four straight lines without taking their pen off the paper and see how they do.

Invariably they are working within the structure of the square rather than realising that it would be quite permissible to extend the line out of the square in order to complete the task. If they have seen this before or even if they haven't, I then move on to asking them to do the very same thing with three straight lines.

This foxes most and the answer is to start with the top left dot and extend the line horizontally to the right and keep going until you can use the earth's curvature to come back on yourself and go through the second line of dots and then using the same idea to come back again and complete the task.

Finally I ask them to do the task with one straight line. The answer is to use a very thick pen!

It's interesting that a lot of people get number three because they've finally got themselves *thinking outside the box*.

Now immediately following this you apply the thinking to the very thing that the coaching session needs to cover. The brain has now reset itself to 'thinking laterally' and will engage in a totally different way compared with the moment just before the 9 Dot coaching tools were applied.

Strategy Tools

1. The Money Pie

This coaching device is useful to both a sole trader or indeed any size of business. The classic challenge is about creating more cash. A coaching session could commence with drawing a circle and the creation of a money pie where good questions lead to open and creative minds as to where a certain sum of money will emerge from in a given time period.

I've often forced the issue in going through this with businesses that want to just talk big concepts or leave the nitty-gritty to other departments or another time. Yet when the session concludes there are smiles in the room and a new sense of 'we can do it'. The other thing about using a pie map in a session is that once the map starts to be built, previously latent ideas start to surface.

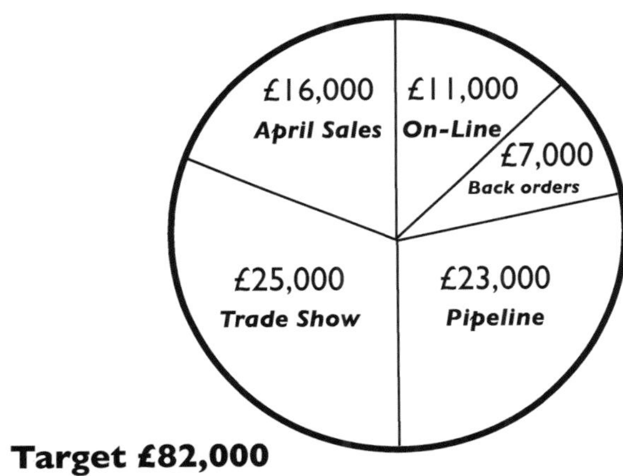

2. The Marketing Engine

Imagine at the heart of every business is an engine constructed to bring new trade through the door. In a business coaching scenario it's good to ask the Board how many routes there are to market. There should be at least four, a bit like four pistons in a basic combustion engine, and ideally six which may be considered the maximum number. Where there are no hard and fast rules for the smaller business it's an interesting concept to get your head around in creating a basic marketing strategy. So minimum four, maximum six. Yet in working with SMEs or small to medium size enterprises, a number of them were working on only two and three piston engine businesses. When they were encouraged to create a four-piston business, the future sales funnel started to look much more exciting. I would normally draw six pistons on a flipchart and start to label them. Sometimes people call out the names of pistons which have never been considered before. It's a great exercise for any business to action and can be done in a matter of a few minutes.

3. The In/On Strategy

The initial concept comes from Michael Gerber and his great question: "Are you working in your business or on it?"

In other words are you being operational – just doing it, or strategic – looking at the bigger picture and where the business is headed. So the In/On Strategy works with individuals as well as teams, departments and the board of a company itself. Is the financial director working in the money or on it? Is the sales director working in the sales or on them? This question may be applied throughout any business. Not only do I want an answer to this question with business clients, I also want percentages. What percentage of time is the sales director actually working on the creation of future sales as opposed to in the sales where he might be doing some of the selling; probably not a good idea for this individual. You may also use this techique in personal coaching:

- Is your client working in their money or on their money?
- In their problems or on their problems?
- In their relationship or on their relationship?
- In their life or on their life?

4. O.D.E. Optimal – Desirable – Essential

Jonathan Streeton introduced this useful coaching lever to me a number of years ago and I've been able to adapt it in all sorts of coaching situations. It's normally used in a negotiation strategy when you go into the negotiation with your essential requirement but also know your desirable outcome, the next best thing to essential and finally your optimal outcome that would mean 'champagne time'. In any kind of goal-getting session, you may also use ODE. In any particular goal, what would be essential, desirable and optimal? So whether it be sales, negotiation or goal getting, having three levels of success broadens options and makes it easier to win.

Performance Tools

1. Prepared Nuggets

This little gem has been a life saver for many people including myself. I first used it when I was at school doing my French oral exam. My French teacher at the time Peter Morley, was a great guy, though his spoken French was not his forte to say the least. When it came time for 'A' Levels I was wondering how I would ever get through the spoken exam. Then I had a a brainwave. I decided to prepare in advance a whole conversation about a subject that the examiner was most unlikely to know about. Given the specialist nature of the topic, I realised I could possibly get away with chatting away with my prepared speech and not having to interact with questions that I would probably not understand. My topic? I chose 'Les Soucoupes Volantes' or Flying Saucers. As soon as the examiner asked: "How are you?", which I would understand, I replied in French: "Very well thank you but very busy with my new interest."

I think you realise the next question she asked which allowed me to unleash my prepared barrage of prepared fluent French that meant the examiner couldn't get a word in edgeways. I can also tell you I got an A.

So how is this a coaching tool?

Often rising stars in businesses are too modest, shy or retiring to be more vocal in meetings and part of the challenge is not being spontaneous enough and the fear of putting their foot in it. If they were to go in with these prepared nuggets, when the time was appropriate they could unleash them to the great delight and perhaps surprise of many of their colleagues. Sales people could benefit by these, as well as introverts who sometimes are not sure what to say to people, all they have to do is a little bit of preparation. One such nugget I helped produce with a senior manager from a well-known confectionery company. The need arose from her being constantly pestered by colleagues throughout the day who she ended up helping to the detriment of her own performance. The prepared nugget she used was a polite: "I would love to help you and I can't because..."

I got her to rehearse, practise and rehearse again until it was second nature for her to say this. I rather think it turned her performance around because for the first time she was able to get on with her own work without having to prop up everyone else who probably now went off and bothered someone else.

2. The Declutter

It's an accepted fact that the more your mind is cluttered with ideas and thoughts the more your performance is likely to suffer. Equally if you can narrow your thoughts to between three and seven subjects at any given period you're more likely to be able to attain better performance.

George A Miller originally published an article in *The Psychological Review* in 1956 concerning the magic number 7 plus or minus 2. It related to a limit in the number of things our brain could focus on at any one time. Miller deduced that the actual number of items was between 5 and 9. In more recent times psychologists seem to have agreed that this initial figure is on the high side and what is more realistic is 5 plus or minus 2. This means a minimum of 3 to a maximum of 7 things we can put our minds to at any one time. There is also the quip about 3 being for males and 7 for females. This relates to many practical things like bullets in a powerpoint presentation.

If you have more than 7 points in the slide you will probably lose your audience. In a similar vein if your slide has 2 points this is less interesting than if it has 3.

How all this relates to decluttering is that the more there is of anything the less we will get from understanding, using or capitalising upon it. Decluttering helps because it creates more space both visually and mentally. It's a commitment I love my coachee to have on their list of things they need to complete before the end of any initial coaching. Decluttering ranges from desks, workstations, whole offices, the car, one's home and so on. "If in doubt throw it out" is often a useful mantra because space encourages the feeling of freedom, and freedom of thought brings large helpings of personal creativity.

3. The Chicken Task

A great challenge tool is *The Chicken Task* and is all about daring your client to do something that they know they need to, but have been too chicken to take any action on to date. By calling it a 'chicken task' it infers it's more important to achieve than an ordinary one and demands more courage which is the challenge. Enough said.

4. Voicemail Performance

Some of the things that say a lot about you may include your choice of pen, the shoes you wear, the watch on your wrist, the handbag or briefcase you carry and that highly neglected one – your voicemail message.

Getting your coachee to improve and enhance their personal image in the world could well begin with this little gem.

The majority of people's voicemails are rather dull, abrupt, could-not-care-less, the downside list is pretty long. Very few messages stand out to compliment the owner and in a competitive world a voicemail message is a representation of who the person is. Saying things like: "I'm not here right now," is rather stating the obvious and therefore quite an odd thing to say.

Here is a suggested template that your clients could work from (and perhaps you could use yourself?):

> *Hello this is NAME from COMPANY and thank you for calling. If you would like to leave some contact information I would be delighted to return your call as quickly as possible.*

When you read through this template there initially appears to be nothing magic or amazing about it yet with the right tonality and preferably recorded with a smile, I guarantee it will sound great and people will notice that there is a difference.

This message's benefits include :

1. It's brief and to the point
2. It's friendly and design to create rapport
3. The word 'delighted' makes a big difference to the over all feel of what's being communicated

If you are not keen on it, then think about creating your own, as long it's an improvement on: *I'm not here right now. Leave a message and I'll get back to you. BLEEP.*

When coaching a team, I like to get everyone to re-record their voicemail message at the same time as this will indicate most certainly that there is some evolution going on in this part of the business. It's a soft yet tangible win for everyone and creates an *Immediate Outcome.*

5. Delegation Toolkit

Getting people to delegate well is most certainly something a coach should support and nurture. When a manager or leader for example is able to delegate effectively, it also affects their performance in a positive way.

I would normally explore two types of delegation:

- Garbage dumping
- Motivating plus the realisation of personal potential

It's the latter that good delegation is all about where the delegatee is learning and growing while they support the delegator. To enable someone in a delegation process it's important that:

- they know what you want
- they have the authority to achieve it
- they know how to do it.

It's also important that the delegator keeps in touch from time to time to ensure that all is well and there are no challenges along the way. There's also a point around how the task is passed on. If it's done in a motivational and inspiring fashion the likelihood is that the ultimate result will be infinitely better.

Self-Discovery Tools

1. The Hotel Day

The idea first came to me from an experience I had when I was 14. My English teacher told the class to take a notebook, pen, torch and sit in the garden at dusk and write down every thought that came into their head based on what they heard, saw or felt. That evening before doing this I thought to myself that this was going to be a really short experience and probably a total waste of time. I ended up spending a good hour and a half once I'd started this exercise and could easily have sat there for a further hour at the very least.

Years later I repeated this technique when I took myself away to a hotel where no one could find me and with my blank sheet of paper started to make copious notes of where I was in my life, my business and where I wanted to go in the future. It was an extraordinary event of self-discovery which I repeated on numerous occasions thereafter at regular three to six-monthly intervals.

Coaching people to have hotel days is a great way for them to learn more about themselves and what they need to achieve. The important factors are:

- Hotel or other location where they can sit undisturbed
- No mobile phones at the location or at least switched off
- No one knows where they are so they can't be reached
- Some coaching on how to mind map before they do it

2. 360 Feedback

No, this is not a guerrilla technique and not being suggested. I am proposing that you do a different version of this by first of all losing the term 'feedback'. I always think feedback reminds me of that nasty sound that attacks your ears when a microphone is too close to a speaker. It also reminds me of throwing up for some reason so it's not a word that I relish. Sadly it's also been badly used as a way to beat people up and criticise them where they have to stand there and take it rather like you're supposed to end every hot shower with 60 seconds of freezing cold water.

Recently in a workshop of 12 managers I asked how many of them liked feedback. It wasn't long for about eight hands to shoot up and then I saw a further four people reluctantly raise theirs. When I got down to brass tacks, at least half of the group had to admit they had been brainwashed into accepting the concept that everyone should like feedback because it's good for you. Is it? It's like that quite awful expression *constructive criticism*. Why would anyone want a constructive form of being criticised? Any constructive criticism I've ever heard in my life has been very destructive in nature as it was rarely followed up by any alternatives or on the spot coaching.

So what's the alternative to feedback? It follows in the next coaching lever but for the moment let's stick with how we can get comments from people around us to help us shape our performance and future. One way is to open a Facebook account specifically for this purpose. This is a fun and often much more honest way to get comments from colleagues, friends, family and just about everyone you know. Another way is to have 21 questions and separate them into groups of three and e-mail them to seven people you know. When doing this with a client, it would be good to help them craft the questions and decide who gets which batch of three questions. People receiving three questions by e-mail will probably get them back to you quite quickly. It's when they get a massive 360 degree feedback form that it starts to be an unwieldy and drawn out process.

3. Soulfood

Soulfood is a Caribbean dish and though I've never tasted it, it sounds rather delightful. I also decided to use the term in place of feedback because surely it's about feeding someone's soul in a positive way. In fact soulfood has become so successful when deployed in organisations it underlines the fact that there appears to be a big requirement for more of the positive.

Soulfood is about giving comments or praise to somebody where the information is 'GPS':

- genuine
- positive
- specific

So it's not about just saying 'well done'; it's much more than that. If you have something critical to say about somebody then you shouldn't use Soulfood.

Remember that soulfood is not supposed to be another word for feedback. Whoever you coach must absolutely ensure that they're following the three musts at all times: positive, genuine and specific.

"One of the main ingredients lacking in the business world is giving recognition. When it's authentic it has a powerful impact." (Graham Alexander)

Creativity Tools

1. Mind Maps

Over the decades Tony Buzan's clever yet simple-to-use idea has undoubtedly revolutionised learning, problem solving, creativity and note taking.

How to Mind Map

- Turn the paper so it's landscape.
- Have some coloured pens.
- Start in the centre of the page drawing a circle or shape and within it write the title of your mind map.
- Draw your first branch in colour from the centre to the one o'clock position.
- Write in capitals along the first branch the subject or heading for this part of the map.

For example if your map is about traffic congestion this branch could say *top cities where congestion is worst.*

- Notice we're going by a clock face starting at the one o'clock position and branches will then form clockwise so you can read them in an order.
- At the end of your branch have twigs emerge which are sub-points of the main heading. On these twigs you should write in lowercase.

- Continue to be colourful with your map and add pictures, diagrams and sketches to help you remember what the branches and twigs were all about.

Go back to Chapter 4 to see a mind map.

2. Creativity Tips

Apparently because of the way our brains are wired up, when you want to be more creative you should look up and to your right and also whilst doing this take your tongue and press it into the space at the back of your front teeth. I'm not sure these tools are scientifically proven though I have used them successfully myself and passed them on to many coachees who have agreed in the main that they work. All in the mind? Definitely!

3. Perceptual Positioning

To help people be more creative, the use of Perceptual Positioning is an extremely valuable aid. Perceptual Positioning is largely used where there may be a disagreement between two parties who are both looking for a mutually agreeable solution. Typically you look at the world through your eyes and see how you feel, think and what you hear from the other party. The whole thing is repeated where you now put yourself in the shoes of the other party and see it entirely from their perspective. Finally you become an observer and you go through the same conversation again yet now you're observing the two people in conversation and therefore would be perceiving things from a third party point of view. When we add new dimensions to our current perspective we learn new ways of behaving that will enrich and enhance relationships around us. In creativity, Perceptual Positioning is also extremely useful in exploring the relationship between company and customer, employees and customers, company and suppliers and so on. Until you can put yourself in the shoes of others involved in a particular scenario you will never fully appreciate the big picture.

Set Skills

The Set Skills intervention as it suggests is broken down into a number of areas such as sales, customer care, leadership, social media marketing, communication, presentations etc. To give you a taste, I'm going to select Sales and Time Control. What you carry in your coaching arsenal for set skills is your own decision.

Sales

1. The NPR Call

NPR stands for *no particular reason* and it's a great little device for clients who are leaders, managers in sales or do something where networking would be of great value. An NPR call is where they would make between two and four calls every day to people they know for no particular reason. When coaching I create this as a new habit that the client needs to be committed to carrying out. Of course in conversations, sales or networking opportunities inevitably emerge. Alongside this there's another type of call, *The Chicken Call*. This is very much like the Chicken Task yet specifically around making calls to people that the individual knows they should connect with yet are afraid to pick up the phone and make contact.

2. The 'How Close' Technique

Great for sales or negotiation, it's normally used around price. When coaching at Digicel in Jamaica, sales teams were staggered how useful this little technique was in price negotiations with customers. When a customer objected to price rather than say "How much could you afford?" instead the adviser would ask "How close could you get to my offer?"

The words 'how close' take the customer nearer to the offer mentally rather than miles away from the desired amount with words like 'afford'.

3. What do Companies Sell?

This is another marvellous coaching lever for salespeople. When you remind people what all companies really sell suddenly light bulbs go on and breakthroughs are made. Normally a salesperson would respond:

- products
- services
- myself
- my company
- great deals
- goodservice
- relationships

The answer is in fact *feelings*. In sales coaching scenarios I spent a 45-minute guerrilla session centering on this one single idea because when you sell feelings you're probably selling exactly what all customers have at the very top of their shopping list. What and how this actually works for the salesperson would be between coach and coachee.

4. Reciprocity

Coaching clients to use reciprocity in selling offers great advantage to them in the long term. Giving to receive is as old as the Bible. So is what goes around comes around. Today with social media networking and marketing, giving first and selling way down the line is the new way to do business. However it's based on a principle as old as time itself. The challenge is getting salespeople to realise its value today is just as important as it's always been.

Time Control

Time management is a very strange term. Why would anyone ever want to manage their time? Surely it's about controlling and leading it and with this in mind here are some time tools that you could offer clients when appropriate.

1. Parkinson's Time Law

Probably the most famous time tool of all, it states that:

> *Work expands so as to fill the time available for its completion...*

When setting times for meetings you're probably asking for trouble. A one-hour meeting is likely to last at least an hour if not longer. The coaching advantage with Parkinson's Time Law would be to get people to negotiate time down with themselves or others whenever they're planning events or booking appointments in their diary. Also the idea that by getting all the business done in the shortest possible time people go away with bonus time that they were not expecting which is as valuable as coming away with a cheque for a sum of money.

2. Time Foraging

Looking out for 'time pockets' that occur during the day when you least expect them should be used to advantage rather than squandered. Having a list of small things to do may then be applied to these time opportunities when for example a meeting is cancelled, a client is late and you are kept waiting or you're commuting on a train or plane. There are plenty of time opportunities that you can 'forage for' and use to your advantage. Foraging is also thinking ahead of time pockets coming your way on a particular day and being aware of how you will best use this added bonus.

3. The Mad Six Minutes

Mentioned briefly already, here it is again.

The setting aside of a small number of minutes and doing a task at twice the normal speed has two functions:

- It will get you to like what you're doing to the point of wanting to do more of it. The adrenaline released also helps.
- As you know you've only got six minutes you tend to pack more into that time than you would in an ordinary set of six minutes.

To use this to best effect, do use a timing device.

4. The New To-Do List Strategy

To-do lists are very good places to stack lots of things that need actioning. If you are scrupulous about ploughing through the list, the chances are you will be doing a lot of things that you may never have actually needed to do at all. This means a waste of your most valuable resource.

There is another way. Get your coachee to consider that their To-do list is for things that are *not urgent or important*. Urgent and important items should go straight into one's diary where they are diarised against a time for their completion.

This means that things that go on the To-do list should simply be reviewed from time to time and in the fullness of time the chances are many of these items become unnecessary and may be removed from the list altogether. Imagine all the time now saved from *not doing these items.*

7

UNORTHODOX PERFORMANCE STRATEGIES

Fifth Tumbler – Location

Imagine sitting in a warm climate with beautiful weather sipping a cool glass of freshly squeezed tropical fruit juice to also have a coaching session with your coach about the rest of your life – or doing the same exercise in a tiny office without windows with strip lighting and a hard chair to sit on. For years I have been aware that the location in which you choose to coach can have a massive impact on the outcome of the coaching.

Here are some of my favourite coaching locations that I've enjoyed using:

- Chelsea Football Club
- BAFTA in London
- Palace of Westminster
- The London Eye
- The Athenaeum Club
- Elstree Aerodrome
- Albert Square on the set of BBC's EastEnders

- Champneys Health Club
- The British Museum
- Universal Studios, Orlando

Thinking of *Location* playing a part in coaching will still be considered by many as an unorthodox performance strategy. Yet there are so many stunning examples of truly unorthodox strategies, where location played an essential part in creating a great result.

Like the invitation to over 250 business people in Manchester to attend a 'business seminar' given by the then lead conductor of the Berlin Philharmonic Orchestra on stage in a theatre.

He started the main session by inviting four young classical musicians on stage and asked if one of them would mind being 'coached'.

Eventually an 18-year-old female cellist agreed and he asked her to play her best to the audience using sheet music. (None of this was in any way rehearsed).

So she began, and he cajoled her more and more as she played, sometimes raising his voice to get her to really 'go for it'. The audience could see that it was not really working. Then he pointed to her hair tied up in a bun and asked if she would remove the elastic holding it in place. As she did so, she shook her head to use her hair and he used an audible 'anchor' at the moment this happened. Now he asked her to play again, but this time he also asked her to 'free her hair' while playing so that her head movement and his audible anchor, were all rolled into one. The audience could see that her head movement was in fact a powerful catalyst as she shut her eyes and seemed to forget the sheet music. Eventually what came from her was truly amazing, and her three fellow musicians also joined in with equal fervour. They took the girl's lead in playing from their hearts not their heads.

Within minutes the audience was on their feet and at the end of the piece the auditorium erupted in a sea of beaming faces with loud applause.

In the movie *Dead Poets Society* Robin Williams plays an English teacher, where something similar happens. Williams helps an introvert kid evolve into becoming a poet in a few magical minutes by taking him out of his school desk to stand on a small stage almost blindfolded and then 'moved' in a circle and through distraction he encouraged him to spontaneously create poetry from his heart. The kid did just that and the class was stunned.

One of the best collection of unorthodox performance strategies on television that was created over 10 years ago, also proved without any shadow of a doubt that latent potential resides within all of us and provided we choose to find it, then use it, the resulting outcomes are quite simply staggering.

As ever, location was very much at the heart of all the coaching. Channel 4's 'Faking It' TV series hit British screens at the turn of the new millennium. It was soon a smash hit which also won it many awards. Based on the very simple premise that if you were to take someone from a particular occupation, with the right coaching and a time span of thirty days you could get that individual to pass themselves off in a completely new occupation as if they've been doing it for years. From a guerrilla perspective there is no surprise here for me, which is why 'Faking It' is such a shining example about human possibility. That it is possible for anyone to achieve virtually anything if their heart and desire to achieve is sealed in the venture. Plus one further caveat: that they're coached with the right tools and style.

A great example of 'Faking It' was an episode where a student called Alex, normally devoid of any type of aggression, was coached to become a London club doorman. He ended up fooling all the judges when he was interviewed and compared with three other professional doormen in a one-night-only competition. Equally there was also the fake cordon bleu chef, coached by Gordon Ramsay, who won a competition against other real cordon bleu chefs in a remarkable turn of events. No one saw him as the fake which is staggering given that thirty days earlier his culinary expertise centred around being able to make hamburgers from his mobile van at football matches. His double success also included the fact that he ended up winning first prize!

Then there was the Manchester-based courier cyclist who was whisked away and coached to become a polo player in just a month. It was fascinating to observe his fear when he mounts the horse for the first time, yet twenty nine days later he's playing polo and riding horses as if he'd been doing it for at least a decade.

Sadly there was the Yorkshire lass who was coached to become a debutante. This is where it got interesting for me because as I watched the episode I realised that the lady in question was not fully committed to her objective. She turned up at her coach's house wearing trainers and really pushed back on various aspects of the coaching. It was no surprise therefore to see that she failed to pass as a debutante and I wondered why she had even bothered volunteering for the show in the first place.

It's fascinating to take the elements of 'Faking It' apart in order to appreciate what all of us have the potential to achieve.

1. Time Span

Thirty days is a relatively short space of time to learn anything new yet the majority of the contestants in 'Faking It' succeeded in knowing enough and having the confidence to pass themselves off in a completely different career as a seasoned professional.

2. Self-Belief

There's also no question that 'Faking It' contestants all hit a point in their learning process where they felt they either couldn't go on any further or were simply not achieving the results they'd hoped for. Yet despite this they ultimately were able to follow through and win.

3. Perception is Projection

Once individuals were able to truly perceive themselves in their new guise, the ability to subsequently project themselves to the world became much easier.

4. The Coaching that Made All the Difference

Equally passionate about success was a group of three coaches. Each coach had a speciality and in working with the contestant, this group of mentors created a close bond with the coachee that often made the difference in levels of self-confidence with the challenge facing them.

5. No Failure, just Experience

Each 'Faking It' subject also had an opportunity of trialing their new identity in a situation a few days before the final judged event. Some found their world crashing about their ears when they realised that they simply weren't ready yet. Yet the coaching process was about a 50-50 relationship where all coaches took joint responsibility with the coachee. In the main, coaches would look at what was working first rather than making a list of what wasn't.

6. Not Just Looking the Part, but Living It

It was all about living, eating and breathing the new way of being, and doing it absolutely.

7. Practical, Fast and Focused

All the coaching tended to be of a practical nature where the coachee was hardly given any time to focus on anything other than to become more knowledgeable or more experienced in their new profession. Speed once more was a major ingredient.

More and more these days coaches are finding themselves approached by clients that want rapid, targeted and intensely practical coaching methods that would lead to one hundred percent success.

I invariably use 'Faking It' tools to kick-start the coaching process. These tools include Fast Forward, High 5, Mind Changers and State Changers, all of which you will already have read about.

Here's what I want you to do now:

Look at the numbers in the diagram below carefully and you'll see there are three boxes going across the page.

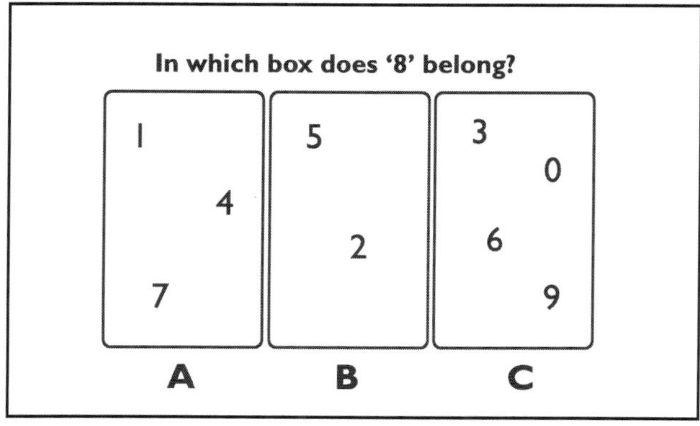

My question is – In which box does '8' go? A, B or C?

The most important question once you've decided, is why that box?

This puzzle was apparently given to two university professors, one who specialised in pure maths and the other statistics. They each took this away over a weekend and returned on the Monday morning to present their findings to the researchers. Curiously neither had come up with the right answer even though each of them had worked out their own reasoning for why they had placed the number '8' in a particular box and both of them also agreed that the answer they were tendering was not a satisfactory one.

This same puzzle was then taken to a primary school and a class of six-year-olds. Within thirty seconds of being asked the question: "Where does the '8' go?" the correct answer came through loud and clear. "Box C"

The answer is Box C, because the number '8' is curvy like the other numbers in the box. In the first box all the numbers are straight and in the second they are curvy and straight.

It appears that the nature of thinking in adults is a predilection to seek out complexity rather than look for simplicity. Why do we always want to make things more complicated than they are or believe that the answer to a question has to be a complex one?

Some of the greatest discoveries ever made were from thinking simple and obvious rather than convoluted and elaborate.

Ockham's Razor is a principle of a theory from the 14th century theologian William of Ockham that states *the simplest explanation is most likely to be the correct one.*

It reasons that when looking for a hypothesis it makes more sense to choose one with the fewest new assumptions. So in the case of the above number boxes puzzle, using Ockham's Razor the explanation requiring the fewest assumptions is shape. Simplicity in our thinking will also lead us to consider shape as the solution.

Simplicity has and always will be a strong resource and catalyst for getting things done. The principle of simplicity is in no way unorthodox though the use of it often is.

The Coach Approach

In order cross reference and compare other performance strategies, particularly unorthodox ones, it would be useful to outline where guerrilla coaching sits in comparison with other support systems.

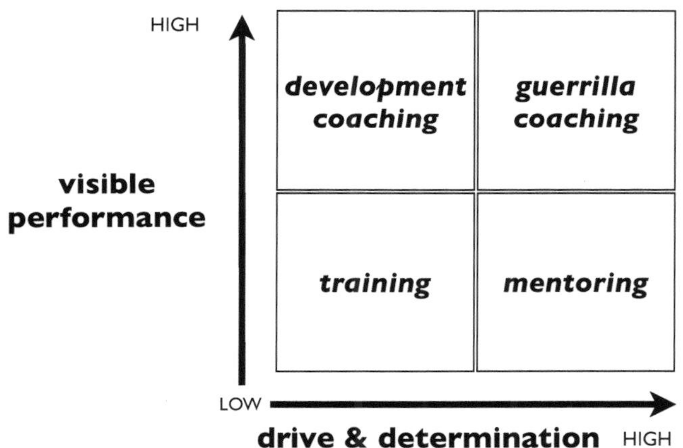

You will see from this matrix that the higher the performance, coupled with the greater the drive and determination, the more appropriate it is to use Guerrilla Coaching as the achievement catalyst. High performers who are essentially lazy or lack confidence probably require more traditional development coaching whilst those with the greatest drive and determination also known as passion, probably need someone to take them in hand such as a mentor. Though guerrilla coaching and its many components may be used for any type of personal effectiveness and human development, the core guerrilla methodology thrives in the top right box of this Boston Matrix where speed is invariably a crucial element.

The Ideal Guerrilla Coach

You will see here from the diagram, the various layers that make the ideal Guerrilla Coach but let's also look at the ideal performer.

The Peak Performer

Looking at the various layers that would be needed to help any performer reach their peak, we notice that the zenith of this diagram is mental toughness. With zero tolerance on one side and mental toughness on the other just imagine being able to bring these two factors together in order to climb K2 or reach the South Pole on foot. Then apply the same thinking to other tasks like getting a better position in your company, making a business more successful or winning hearts and minds with an amazing piece of writing.

In the various Peak Performer layers most are very straightforward, though I'd like to make a quick mention of flex and stretch-ability for an individual who's prepared to do something a different way if the ways they've attempted so far haven't worked.

The layer called 'Knock Down Immunity' is about people who will get up when knocked down time and time again until they eventually achieve what they desire.

So what is the most important layer? I suggest it's mental toughness and perhaps it would be useful to introduce a past client called Kevin O'Rourke. A man who really understands mental toughness.

Mental Toughness – One Reality

Kevin O'Rourke is an 'Ironman'. In 2010 he did the Ironman in Bolton consisting of a 2.5 mile swim followed by a 112 mile bike ride and then a 26.2 mile run.

Not content with this, Kevin is currently looking to qualify for the Marathon Ultra that's called the *Badwater Ultra Marathon* and is the hardest 'ultra' in the world held in Death Valley California.

It's a 135 mile run in 50c degree heat and massive humidity. Recognised globally as 'the world's toughest foot race', this legendry event brings together approximately ninety of the world's toughest athletes, runners, tri-athletes, adventure racers and mountaineers running against each other as well as the elements. It covers this staggering 135 miles non-stop from Death Valley to Mount Whitney California and is the most demanding and extreme running race offered anywhere on planet Earth.

Whilst anyone can enter the Ironman, it takes more than a mere marathon runner to finish it. To enter the event you have to have completed at least three 100-mile non-stop runs in a time less than

24 hours and preferably in high temperatures. They do not consider standard Ironman races as tough enough!

It's really worth a little bit more information around Kevin's ordeal as mental toughness is something that guerrilla coaching deems as a powerful success ally. But what is it? Mental Toughness is a collection of techniques which can be used together or individually and include:

1. What's Next Thinking. When you've surmounted one hurdle rather than think of the pain of what you've just experienced, you get yourself into already thinking *so what's next?*
2. See emotional and physical pain as non-requirements to success. Most champion athletes have to get themselves into a zone where there is no pain. Achieve this through practice and the athlete will be able to go much much further. Going back to karate style board-breaking, those candidates who punch through the wood with confidence and speed feel nothing. Those that lack the confidence and harbour doubt or fear end up slapping the wood and stinging their hands.
3. Get used to doing unfamiliar things. Take different routes to places, different forms of transport, make unfamiliar food and drink choices, because when you really test yourself and/or your body you will be faced with many unfamiliar feelings and emotions. The automatic thinking is to stop. It takes mental toughness to push through regardless.
4. Use mental imagery. Disassociating yourself from what is going on, maybe seeing someone else running and you are simply watching from the sidelines through mental imagery will make a difference. It would also help if you see yourself strong, winning and unstoppable.
5. Focus on what you want, not on what you don't want, but avoid over-focusing
6. Expect the unexpected and prepare for this the best you can both practically and mentally
7. Harbour an insatiable thirst for success that cannot be quenched. The use of Mind Changers before hand is vital.

"Mental toughness is not being affected by anything but what's going

on in the game no matter what spectators, other players, or referees are doing. It's being able to block out what's not important and focus solely on what is." (Jenny Brenden, Women's Basketball Champion)

Here's more of Kevin's account on his latest expedition using mental toughness:

> *"The Ironman was hard but the Ultra, which took place four weeks later, was the toughest. The most difficult thing was coping mentally, especially with the intense pain, the monotony of running that distance, often through the night and spending lots of time alone with only my thoughts, which I have to say consisted mainly around* ***pulling out****,* ***tiredness*** *and* ***pain****. But my resolve and commitment to finish pulled me through and I would say sheer pig-headedness also helped.*
>
> *I wanted to prove to myself and others that I was still strong both mentally and physically. What really helped was receiving some amazing text messages from team mates at some very low points I experienced. I finished in 26 hours and 17 minutes later where the cut-off for finishing was 28 hours. The standard Ironman cut-off is 17 hours and this year I finished in just 13 hours and 40 minutes.*
>
> *However the Ultra took its toll and I suffered a torn soleus muscle, IT band syndrome and damaged ligaments and cartilage in my right leg.*
>
> *This in turn created massive blisters the size of the palm of my hand which I still had to run on. I received the injury only after 24 miles into the race and still had a further 61 miles to complete. As you would imagine the injury got worse and the more I continued to run, the more the run became a walk and the walk became a crawl to the finish."*

Whatever drives people towards this level of human potential is something all of us could use particularly when we see others stretch themselves to the limit of human endurance and then we compare this with pushing people past the finishing line in their own pursuits that are comparatively easier to tackle and achieve. And when we learn of people like Kevin O'Rourke and remind ourselves of what we are all truly capable of, many of our so-called challenges and barriers to success in life seem to evaporate.

So let's leave mental toughness and look at mental flexibility, using other unorthodox methodologies that are at our disposal. These are often simple, cheap and very effective in their own right. This also flips the idea of 'Location' to be seen from a modern technological perspective. Indeed cyberspace is yet another location.

Guerrilla Results through Social Media

When I introduced this book I referenced *Guerrilla Marketing* and we now appear to have gone full circle and come back to it by exploring social media in coaching.

Social media would initially appear unconnected to One-to-One coaching yet in the world of the guerrilla coach it can be a useful route to rapid results.

Imagine wanting to get a message out to a large group of people in an equally large organisation. Speed and effectiveness would definitely emerge from the smart use of social media technology, not to mention the cohesive interaction of all the members of the group. I first came across this concept in doing a piece of work for Vodafone UK in 2007 that I called *The Red Effect*. This was the first time I ever thought about social media and coaching in the same strategy, and it worked rather well. Delegates were missioned to make discoveries using YouTube and other social media type websites. Although the application was around helping their customers get more from their mobile phones, I also enjoyed using the same methods to enhance the overall coaching experience. More coaches are coaching by phone, text, e-mail, webinars, websites, media and Skype.

Today Facebook and Twitter are great sustainability tools and offer platforms for post workshop follow-up as well as places to collaborate after any learning or discovery. If the coach gets it right then Twitter provides a mini daily 'info-bite' that can become quite addictive for exsiting clients as well as attracting many new ones. At the time of writing, I think it fair to say that the majority of coaches are failing to use social media for all its worth, yet the technology and opportunity it brings that's now available to every coach also offers the unlimited use of video, audio and other combinations which will enhance any coaching methodology in quality and overall effectiveness.

One of the fundamental factors that many coaches have over looked in the past, a blind spot I certainly fell foul of in my early career, was the lack of appreciation for an individual's sensory preferences.

As a visual I would spend so much time drawing pictures and bombarding my clients with visual imagery while totally unaware that I was losing my auditory clients who were being starved of their own primary sensory preference. The use of media can create significant breakthroughs, particularly if you aim to match your client's favourite sensory requirements. Yet a further challenge is the mistaken belief that you may need special knowledge.

Creating Effective Coaching Media

So why would you want to create video media to supplement good coaching? Media is in fact a further take on 'Location'. Coaching can take place on screen or by audio using the stage of the human mind. For this reason, coaching and media can be powerfully linked.

I often use movie clips to guerrilla coach and sometimes even asking a client to watch an entire movie as homework to make powerful points for the next session.

Think about the many occasions when you've been affected by a motivational movie or a fantastic book that's created vivid images in your mind that have moved you to do something you wouldn't normally have done.

The fact is we are all visual to some degree and the visual studio of our minds, when stimulated effectively, make us more aware and offer us deeper insights compared with merely reading information or undertaking face to face coaching alone. You don't need an expensive website to have a fantastic collection of video media; all you need is a YouTube account and ensure you add to your collection regularly.

Actually creating the media for the totally uninitiated is infinitely easier than you may think.

Buying an automatic recording device is a breeze, given that most of us already have one on our mobile phone. Learning to download and edit this material could happen in a single hour at a one-to-one session at Apple for example. Here are some hot tips for even hotter videos:

- Use a tripod whenever possible.
- Edit as much as you can in the camera. Use the pause button between shots and ensure you practise the shots before you film.
- There should be a beginning, middle and end.
- Make sure you have a microphone close to the person speaking at all times. This is sometimes just a camera microphone.
- Always film a title.
- For outdoor work people should be facing the sun.
- Disappointingly short is always preferable than boringly long.
- Consider interviewing clients, especially success stories and use the media to send while coaching others. This can be audio or video.

I have a dedicated hard drive to grow my video collection from various sources and use the media as creatively as possible during guerrilla coaching that invariably adds to the momentum of the overall client experience.

The recording and editing of audio is often even simpler than video.

As an Apple user I recommend Garage Band as the ideal software to create your audios with ease and my top audio suggestion is to invest in a good microphone. If you think about it, it's much easier to create a significant collection of audios than to do the same with video which may involve more time and preparation in filming and editing. Audio therefore could be the ideal way to begin your media collection, and here are some additional tips you may find useful for audio:

- Consider adding a faint backing track to your audios to make them sound more interesting.
- A music intro and outro makes it sound really professional and gives the listener audible start and stop cues.
- Editing out the 'umms' and 'ahhs' makes it sound truly professional.

- Always record an audio from a written script rather than speaking spontaneously unless it's an interview.
- Where a script is concerned, less is definitely more and make it sound conversational rather than read out.

The Audio Special

One further option for the audio is an under used technique that's so easy to do. Think about creating an audio on say your mobile phone and within moments of recording it send it off to a client with a key message. This is a great 'value add', as well as your client feeling that you are thinking about their progress beyond the set agreed sessions.

A further aspect is to record and edit an audio once a week for your top clients where you are featured speaking to them in a 'fast forward' format. They could then download it onto their own mobile device or burn it onto a CD and listen to it in the car.

The above tools are but a handful of the large array of coaching techniques available to any coach who's prepared to step outside the traditional ways of the past and explore the exciting new possibilities of the future. And do consider downloading the free Guerrilla Coaching application in the Apple Apps store.

8

MIND YOUR LANGUAGE

Sixth Tumbler – Experiential

Apart from using as many of the previous tumblers in *The Guerrilla Wheel* as possible, a further suggestion lies in the Sixth Tumbler which is about the coachee's experience starting with the spoken word.

How you say what you say and the manner in which you present your ideas will always polish the final experience for the client quite significantly.

It's the coachee's experience that influences their subconscious level of buy-in and the subsequent quality of their commitment around actions.

In coaching today, most coaching practitioners would see the art of asking great questions and communicating succinctly with clients as essential attributes.

Afterall without these aspects, how could your coaching be effective? Yet the often over looked power of language in coaching and the dynamic use of words to create shades of meaning; delicate nuances that make the difference between a client being partially motivated or permanently inspired.

It's so easy to run sessions with 'word blindness', unaware that you have a much greater power to enrich the coaching. Things like a change in your voice tonality, becoming more positive with the choice of your words, using more assumptive statements about the client's future outcomes and the removal of any negative or 'grey' language. Parents have long been potential culprits who have had the power to scar their children with a throw away line like: "You're being stupid".

How many children have taken this unhelpful comment as a subconscious command?

Similarly, a coach is in a comparable position where the coachee's subconscious can pick up unguarded comments and expressions, even as seemingly innocuous as: "Don't feel bad about it", which will actually have the reverse effect. Or what about "if you manage to achieve this" versus "when you achieve this"?

There have been many experiments around semantic priming or the way words can programme our thinking and one I learned from NLP Master, Matt Snaith was to place two groups of people around two separate flip charts in two separate rooms.

Group 1 would see a collection of single words that were all positive and Group 2 would be looking at words that were largely negative. However the difference in the word groups were subtle rather than glaringly obvious. The teams were asked to make short sentences with these words and they were given 10 minutes. There would also be a small group of observers who would watch the two groups during the exercise and also when the teams came back one by one after the session into the main seminar room.

What would invariably happen is the first group would return smiling, chatting and bouncing in while the second group that had the negative collection of words, would meander their way back, look underwhelmed and even unhappy.

There was no surprise either that the second group only had completed a few sentences that were very negative compared with the first group's much longer list of positive up beat line liners.

Accepting the power and influence of words on the human mind, let me ask you now to think about your deliberate choice of words and phrases when you coach, and if you have not even thought about this before, is it time to review this coaching development opportunity?

When you're coaching, particulary with guerrilla values, you will also be selling notions such as a more positive mindset is the best way forward, be paradign aware when making choices and so on. Your words will be controlling the overall effect or experience.

And equally in sales, the use of quality words is much more likely to raise price perception in the mind of a buyer rather than hearing lower quality or negative words. Welcome to the world of Semantic Priming or influencing feelings and thinking by word choice.

This was scientifically demonstrated on a body language TV series. An experiment was conducted on two different people tasting two bottles of wine with their brains wired up to an EEG. The first taste of wine in bottle 'X' indicated they thought the quality of the wine was from an expensive wine producer because of its taste, while the second wine in bottle 'Y' they viewed less favourably as cheap plonk. Again the EEG supported these convictions with hard evidence. However what they didn't know was that despite different labels, both bottles of wine were exactly the same and the only difference was the words used to describe the wine. The quality of the words chosen had created two totally different cerebral experiences – and this beautifully illustrated both the latent power yet potential danger of semantic priming.

Like electricity, words can be used for good to build, grow and develop someone or sabotage, demean and even destroy a person in things like self esteem and confidence. So how can you change the words you use?

I remember meeting business speaker Peter Thomson chatting to me off stage at an event many years ago. He asked me whether I would want to know if I had suddenly acquired a spot on my nose, or would I be too embarrassed to have this pointed out and instead prefer to discover the fact myself. As I started to rub my nose with embarrassment he smiled and assured me that my nose was fine but there was something I was clearly not aware of in the presentation I had just made. "You said 'erm' eight times."

I shook his hand thanking him for his candour as two things occurred to me. One, very few people would ever tell you your weakness so openly in a helpful way as he had done and I appreciated it. Two, now I knew it, how would I fix this communication fraility?

The remedy I used I have also subsequently used with hundreds of clients and again it's the use of the elastic band on the wrist technique. Other ways of fixing communication glitches are reminders on index cards that you can read everyday. This will code your subconscious with more powerful words and phrases over time. So the use of well-chosen words in language is an important factor in successful guerrilla coaching. Words create pictures that stimulate the imagination, and the imagination in turn creates the feelings and emotions that dictate the likelihood of major actions following the words.

Neuro-linguistics is also very much about the use of language to influence outcomes and though the jury is out in traditional coaching circles about the use of NLP as a coaching tool, I believe it has a place if used with integrity.

The usual bone of contention for its use with clients is the suggestion that NLP is something subversive and we've all seen masters like Paul McKenna and Derren Brown use it very effectively in TV shows for entertainment purposes. It's my firm belief that in the hands of a good coach, neuro-linguistics can positively help to influence a client in doing more right things as well as make the right decisions to get to where they want to go quickly. Also given that no one can be hypnotised against their will, NLP is no more coercive than television advertising. In short, NLP can give the guerrilla coach a powerful edge and useful coaching advantage that can benefit the coachee enormously. Some of the ways language and neuro-linguistics benefit include:

- Creating rapport
- The removal of mental barriers
- Creating the desire to take action
- Deleting fear and phobias
- Better decision making
- Motivation and inspiration
- An appreciation of latent human potential

Fundamental Language Tools

The VAKAD factor

Appreciating that we have a predilection for a primary sensory communication style such as visual, auditory, kinaesthetic or auditory digital, then it makes sense that there is an advantage in choosing the right style to match a client's language preference.

As a visual myself, I'm very much at home when the following words are used:

See	*Focused*	*Ray*	*Illuminate*
Look	*Hazy*	*Mesmerise*	*Twinkle*
Appear	*Crystal clear*	*Watch*	*Clear*
View	*Flash*	*Perspective*	*Foggy*
Show	*Imagine*	*Frame*	*Snapshot*
Dawn	*Picture*	*Shine*	*Vivid*
Reveal	*Sparkling*	*Dim*	*Perceive*
Envision	*Observe*	*Image*	*Light*
Vision		*Vision*	

For auditories they are probably more at home with:

Hear	*Silence*	*Attune*	*Babble*
Listen	*Be heard*	*Outspoken*	*Echo*
Sound(s)	*Resonate*	*Tell*	*Orchestrate*
Make music	*Deaf*	*Announce*	*Whisper*
Harmonise	*Mellifluous*	*Talk*	*Snap*
Tune in/out	*Dissonance*	*Speak*	*Hum*
	Overtones	*State*	*Loud*
	Unhearing	*Whine*	*Dialogue*

For the kinaesthetics (emotions and feelings) these might be preferred:

Feel	*Throw out*	*Touch base*
Touch	*Turn around*	*Impression*
Grasp	*Hard*	*Rub*
Get hold of	*Unfeeling*	*Smooth*
Slip through	*Concrete*	*Pushy*
Catch on	*Scrape*	*Stumble*
Tap into	*Get a handle on*	*In touch*
Make contact	*Solid*	*Relaxed*
Cool	*Suffer*	*Loose*
Tepid	*Heavy*	

And for the auditory digitals (logic analysis and making sense of things):

Sense	*Motivate*	*Know*
Experience	*Consider*	*Question*
Understand	*Change*	*Be conscious*
Think	*Perceive*	*Logic*
Learn	*Insensitive*	*Reasonable*
Process	*Distinct*	*Statistically*
Decide	*Conceive*	

I like to make it a practice to ascertain the 'VAKAD' profile (Visual, auditory, kinaesthetic, auditory digital) of my coachee at a very early stage and be conscious of this language pattern when coaching.

The main way the person's profile is attained is through eye movement observation, coupled with getting a sense of who the person is in their word choice and the body language they display. This knowledge becomes very useful when selecting coaching interventions and using a coaching lever like Mind Changers.

'Don't' read this paragraph

Since the brain finds it very difficult to change an image it's already been given, 'don't' often means 'do'.

Don't waste your time
You don't need to worry
Don't forget to complete this before we meet next session
Don't think about this any more

...are some examples.

Positive language does of course need effort and energy, and for many new to coaching this approach may feel a little alien at first.

The Positive Factor

The famous British trait of understatement is probably not helpful in driving teams and individuals to attain ultra-successful results.

Positive language for many is an acquired habit rather than something they can activate from day one. It's largely about who you are and your core beliefs as the tool should only be used by a practitioner who actually says the positive words with genuine conviction.

There is also new evidence to suggest that people who are optimists live approximately eight years longer than their pessimist cousins. I can well imagine this because pessimism produces negative energy and stress which are known killers. The great additional benefit about positive language is that it makes you a more attractive person to the world at large. As human beings we are all attracted to people who exude a positive warm feeling rather than a cold negative one.

Influencing or Coercion?

When I'm working with my personal gym trainer, he's issuing instructions which early on start as polite requests yet as we move closer and closer to achieving the desired target, the requests become positive commands and towards the final home straight there's no room for politeness, and his voice raises - albeit maintaining a positive intention.

Yet attaining the result is a special moment and the euphoric sensation that it is also experienced makes achieving the outcome such a wonderful destination to arrive at. In gym training, traditional coaching wouldn't work. In addition, if the trainer took a more non-directive approach, where perhaps ninety percent of decision making on how far to go was entirely up to the coachee, the chances are, most would complete their routines too early.

Over the years I have thought long and hard about how much influence, versus how much cajoling is appropriate when coaching which in turn will affect word choice.

It's also been fascinating to involve many of my fellow coaches in somewhat playful yet serious discussions about this issue. And though we all believe in getting the best outcome for our client, there's a big division in the thinking around how much influence we should exert. Before you get the wrong idea, this is not about choosing between 'carrot or stick' and holding up the stick as the guerrilla answer. It's about deciding how far you should go in deciding how much influence you should bring to bear and therefore how much store you will place on communication style and word choice as tools from your coaching kit. Before offering a possible answer let's look at some more aspects around NLP.

More Neuro-linguistic 'technology' in coaching

The Pain and Pleasure of Nominalisations

One of the disappointments in NLP is the terminology and gobbledegook often associated with it. I normally get quite a negative response whenever I raise the question in NLP circles as to why the language used is so complex and convoluted? It seems to fly in the face of NLP values of clarity and simplicity. Given it would be inappropriate for me to create new names for these things, the best I can do is to offer simple 'translations' for some really useful tools.

Nominalisations

A nominalisation is an expression using a noun which should in fact be a verb.

People name something as a noun in order to use it as an excuse or to hide behind it.

The nominalised expression *I have a lot of fear* would be better expressed *there's one thing that makes me afraid (and that's not planning sufficiently)*.

Here are some more:

- Stress is getting me down – *I love to de-stress in the gym*
- Communication in my team is bad – *we are communicating our differences to improve team morale*
- Sales have slumped – *we are selling in new markets*
- Marketing has got harder – *we are marketing in new ways*

Here we make the noun into a verb and add a positive reframe. It works a treat.

When you're coaching and able to spot these nominalisations, you're also able to take your client to task in their expression of something in vague or wolly terms.

De-nominalising would involve turning the noun back into a verb as seen in the earlier examples which lay bare the facts of the situation and allows the client to realise they must take more responsibility for the solution. They are then no longer 'hiding' in the safety of the noun.

When you hear someone nominalise about fear for example, it's good to ask questions such as:

- What aspect of this do you fear?
- Who's afraid?
- Why do you say fear?
- Where does this fear you mention come from?

The opposite approach is also true, you can turn a verb such as "I'm afraid" into a nominalisation to create a form of dissociation or desensitisation between the person who's afraid and the experience itself as in: "Now I understand what I'm afraid of, it's a fear I can walk away from."

"Incorrect use of language leads to incoorect thinking."
Buckminster Fuller

Spotting the Positive Intention

Somewhat controversial, there's an idea that at some level all behaviour started off as a positive intention. Another way to express this is that all behaviour serves or did serve at some point in time a positive purpose.

Some would argue that this is merely reframing, yet as a coach if you always think of someone's negative behaviour as possibly starting off as having a good or positive intent behind it, then perhaps you can get to the root cause of a matter more easily and less judgementally.

I was once working with a lady who appeared to lack all drive and motivation around her career until I dug deeper looking for the positive intention. Eventually I discovered that she loved and respected her parents so much that she would never ever do anything to destroy that connection she had with them.

This resulted in her not wanting to make more money or have a higher social position than her parents had achieved in their professional lives which consequently had a major impact on her level of ambition going forward.

I suggested that she have a conversation with her parents and this eventually did the trick. She came back fully renewed and invigorated about the future realising she had the full support of those she loved the most who desperately wanted her to succeed in ways they never had never had the opportunities to do.

The Three Mental Filters – a quick summary

Thought is normally subjected to a three pronged subconscious filtering process: generalisation, distortion and deletion that are normally influenced by pre-existing beliefs and may often include memories of the past. In coaching, being filter-aware is important in order to challenge belief-based barriers and unhelpful paradigms.

Generalisation

When working in the United States, someone asked me about the beefeaters in London. My own generalisation was around the word 'beef' and therefore first started thinking of a chain of restaurants that served good steaks. The American's generalisation however was that the beefeaters synonymous with the Tower of London actually roamed the streets a bit like parking enforcement officers, complete in their red tunics carrying pikestaffs.

We do love to generalize and put things in boxes don't we? Of course the brain does this to create less stress in having to know what to do with all the thoughts we have. In coaching, generalisation by either client or the coach can easily lead to misunderstandings and mistakes in communication.

Distortion

This normally happens where people jump to conclusions. They are distorting the true nature of reality and what they're seeing with their own eyes. If you're watching a youth in a hooded garment running along the street closely followed by a police officer, the normal distortion would be to connect these two events together and suddenly you're looking at cops and robbers. What if you then investigated this incident more closely and realised they were both dashing to an old lady who had fallen in the street? When coaching, by asking lots of good questions you are removing the possibility of distorting the facts that inevitably lead to confusion.

Deletion

This is where you disallow information to enter your thinking for one reason or another. It could easily happen if you're not paying attention when someone is speaking to you. A great example of deletion can be seen on YouTube from an advertisement created by Transport for London. Here a dozen basketball players, some dressed in black and some dressed in white, are playing a game and you're asked to count how many passes the team in the white shirts make. Of course what happens is your attention is so attuned to the white shirt team that you completely delete those wearing the black shirts or anything else on the screen. Whilst this is going on a player dressed as a gorilla, also dressed in black, strolls across the screen from one side to the other. At the end of the video viewers are asked to correctly say how many passes they witnessed, though when you mention the gorilla most have no idea what you're talking about, until of course they see the clip once again.

They deleted all black items while focusing on white shirted players. Deletion happens so often that people miss the obvious. A good coach will help point out the potential deletions and open people's eyes to new possibilities.

All of these filters they are triggered by language.

Adding the Guerrilla Factor

The Embedded Command

One of the best examples of an embedded command is: "You're going to love this."

Embedded commands when used in selling will often tempt the purchaser to go ahead with the proposition. Here is a sales classic: "By now you're probably ready to make the right decision and I want to make sure you're buying with confidence." (*By now* sounds the same as *buy now*.)

These are rather powerful subconscious commands that in coaching – even selling – may appear inappropriate and sometimes they will be.

However using embedded commands with integrity when you're coaching can motivate, drive and focus clients to achieve more and use their personal potential to a higher degree such as:

- "I know you're going to do your utmost to achieve this relatively easy goal."
- "When you build on the successes you're going to achieve, it will make a massive impact on helping you grow your profitable business really fast."
- "I can tell by your passion you're going to sail through any challenge in a way where you'll feel stronger and have greater confidence to achieve even more."

I also rather like: "When now would be a good time to make your first commitment with me?"

I do tend to say this with a smile on my face even though only a small number of people I say it to ever appreciate what I've really just said.

Yes Tags

You would like to know about 'yes tags' wouldn't you? And this is of course how to create a 'yes tag'. Here are some more examples:

- You do don't you?
- You would wouldn't you?
- You should shouldn't you?
- You are aren't you?

When coaching, provided you use a 'yes tag' with positive tonality then it's a useful way to help keep your client forward-focused with sufficient optimism. There are also 'no tags'. I had a Big Issue salesman approach me recently and say, "You wouldn't have two pounds on your for a Big Issue, would you?" I think you know what my answer was.

Coaching Assumptives

Here are three examples key words you may use when coaching, where an assumptive outcome is desired.

- Yet
- Still
- Happy

The first one 'yet' is a great reminder to your client that although they haven't achieved something they will indeed be achieving it in the near future.

"So you haven't made your first million yet?"

The use of the word 'still' is useful when you want to get the client to go ahead or take action with something that they alluded to earlier. For example, they might have said they wanted to start a business soon and intimated that they could start before the end of the month. If we got to the point at which they were seriously thinking about making a decision, rather than ask: "So do you want to do this?" I could say: "Can you still start before next month?"

The assumption is they will be starting the business and I am simply clarifying the date.

The third great coaching word is 'happy'. When asked as a single-word question it's a great shorthand way to get to the heart of the matter in order that a decision is made quickly and instinctively. I could say to a client: "So there are a lot of things to weigh up here but let me ask – do you feel really comfortable going for this goal?" versus a single word: "Happy?"

Brevity is nearly always a better option than high detail.

When coaching sales people and they come out with a whole long list of closing techniques, I simply suggest that they use one short very assumptive and powerful word with their customers after a presentation and that is the question, "Happy?"

It would bring in many more sales.

Metaphors and Stories – enhancing the coaching experience

Central to all effective coaching are metaphors and stories. Whether you are on stage in front of a large audience, working with a team or working one-to-one, the inclusion of metaphors and appropriate stories creates a quality layer that aids comprehension, increases clarity and often ignites inspiration. Normally the stories are real events that the listener gets into and mentally assimilates in a fraction of the time it would take to convey the same message without the story.

Coaching Questions and Requests

Here are some to ponder over and hopefully use:

- If you could only achieve one major future goal,what would it have to be?
- What are the top three breakthroughs you are failing to implement in order to achieve your most important goal?
- Is the child you were proud of the adult you now are?

- Which one aspect of your personality would you like to strengthen in the next 7 days?
- What must happen in your business next to make a major breakthrough?
- What bad habit are you ignoring that if removed, would dramatically transform your future?
- Score your level of happiness out of 10. What has to happen next to increase the score? (It's rarely 10 for anyone.)
- Are you working on your life or just in your life? (Same question for career, health, relationships, partner, money, business, your future)
- If there was another skill you could master immediately what would it be?
- If there was one living person you could chat to right now for insights and help around career/business who would you choose and why?
- If you could go back in time 10 years and advise your past self, what would the advice be? (1, 5, 15, 20 years etc)

Isn't it great that in professional coaching you have the opportunity, to serve others by asking deep, significant and meaningful questions designed to give them wings to fly?

Such questions are made up of smaller segments called words. Minding your language, using the most powerful and appropriate words adds impact for your clients' benefit, and will allow you to make a bigger difference.

'Experiential' must also take into account of something on a much more fundamental level: the physical experience.

This may be achieved in a number of ways, notably by *coach-walking* or getting them to stand and present their thoughts and ideas or doing something practical to illustrate a point. This is more dynamic and interesting than just sitting in the same spot for the entire session.

It's worth reminding yourself as a coach that the original co-achievers were sports people and all the coaching was practical and on the move.

9

GIVING THE MOST TO YOUR CLIENTS

Seventh Tumbler – Sensory

Bringing senses into play and matching clients' preferred sensory styles where possible when coaching has already been underlined. We are all sensory beings and enjoy using all of our senses, particularly in positive situations. The difference this tumbler brings to the guerrilla coaching process is to increase that sensory element in order to maximise the coaching experience which in turn will greatly enhance the chances of overall success.

When I think *coaching session* I also think: "What will the client see, hear, feel, smell and taste?" What effect will this in turn have on them?

Sensory Intent

Sensory experience is mainly guided by the intention of the coach. It's that gut feeling or intuition that's hard to put into words. In any client relationship the essential chemistry must exist for client and coach to feel they are in a proper communication partnership.

When originally creating the *Guerrilla Wheel* I wanted the seventh tumbler to be 'Soul', yet such a word can be misconstrued and even seen as somewhat flaky or 'new age'. I simply wanted to convey the idea that there is something indefinable at work when the right coaching relationship is in place, 'soul' was the word word that came to mind.

What also worked was 'sensory connection' or simply *Sensory.*

Sensory is about conveying the right sensations with the three primary senses in order the other person gets 'good vibes' about the connection. In *Guerrilla Coaching* I suggest this could be by 5 values or underlying principles.

This chapter is about how to best exploit these values in a coaching relationship in order that you give value to your client through a strong connection.

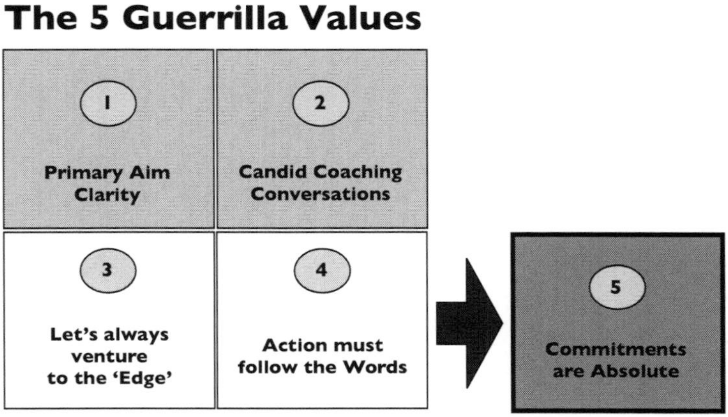

The 5 Guerrilla Values

1 **Primary Aim Clarity**	2 **Candid Coaching Conversations**	
3 **Let's always venture to the 'Edge'**	4 **Action must follow the Words**	→ 5 **Commitments are Absolute**

You see that the first value starts with Primary Aim or the picture your client should hold in mind about their dream life and/or career path for the future. Putting this value to work with each and every client will potentially leverage massive wins, both tangible and intangible, both financial and spiritual and will also include family, health and general well-being.

Primary Aim – the Linchpin to Achieving Goals

The biggest missing piece to the coaching jigsaw is enquiring about someone's Primary Aim. This can be very daunting for both coach and coachee and maybe one of the reasons why it's rare for coaches to dig this deep when asking for a wish list from a client.

If you think about it, stating goals just for the sake of it, is a bit like buying a car because next door has one. Unless you own your dreams you'll certainly never take full responsibility for attaining them.

Linda Westwood was a financial adviser in her mid-fifties and we'd had some initial coaching sessions specifically on helping her to build her ailing client base. Eventually we had to get down to the nitty-gritty and discuss what she truly wanted to achieve. My first question had to be about her Primary Aim. At first she wasn't clear what a Primary Aim was until I fully explained that it was that deep-seated inner desire that usually related to one big compelling and sometimes all-consuming thing; possibly what her entire life was about. After much discussion she eventually raised her hands and said that she now realised what her problem was. She didn't have a Primary Aim and whenever she set objectives they had no real meaning that in turn meant she never fully embraced them, and therefore never achieved them.

At this time she also appeared quite stressed and under a lot of pressure to hit various targets and I suggested that perhaps she should take a brief holiday with one major goal attached. She comes back with her Primary Aim defined.

It was curious how Linda went about taking this time off because apparently she went to a local travel agent known to her and placed her credit card on the counter saying that she was going off to do some shopping and when she returned would they please provide her with a week in the sun somewhere quiet.

This underlined her state of mind at the time, not even being able to decide on a destination for a few days away. When Linda returned the travel agent had already set out a schedule and had purchased a return ticket to the island of Captiva off the coast of Florida. Within days she was jetting out to this laid back beauty spot that was small on people and big on tranquility. It was a perfect place to unwind.

Then something interesting happened. With the words 'Primary Aim' very much in her mind she started to explore the island and eventually found herself walking on a beach only to see a wonderful looking house 'on stilts' spilling onto the beach.

The most interesting fact about it was the 'For Sale' sign on the front gate. That very day she had the real estate agent take her inside for a proper look and this is when the real magic happened. As she walked through the main door, into the large lounge area and caught sight of the deep blue ocean, her inner voice said: "You're home".

For the first time in her life Linda Westwood had discovered something that really grabbed her soul in an over-powering sensory experience. She described it as a state of joy mixed with schoolgirl excitement. Her gut feeling was that she longed for a different yet fully visioned future; a future with new possibilities and one set on this island that she wanted to spend the rest of her life on.

To Linda's self astonishment and the surprise of the real estate agent, she found herself offering the full asking price and a few days later, on the plane home she had already worked out a plan as to how she was going to get this unexpected yet most important future goal in her life.

By the time we had our next session she was a new woman and I wasn't the only one to notice the evolution. Friends, family and other business associates all saw a new Linda Westwood and she ended up having one of her best business months ever Yes, she had also discovered her Primary Aim.

In the movie *The Shawshank Redemption* the Primary Aim of our wrongly convicted hero is to attain his freedom from incarceration.

It takes nearly 20 years, but he achieves it in the most spectacular fashion. I mention this movie because I often ask my coachee who is considering what their Primary Aim could be to watch it as 'homework'. For many who see it, it's one of the most inspirational movies they have ever seen.

I was once coaching someone, early on in my career, who massively increased their income in a very short space of time. Years later they reported in the media on how they initially had no idea of how they were going to achieve one of their most important goals that they did manage to attain yet mused that their coach at the time, (me), had no idea either. But they missed the point completely, and I take full responsibility for the fact. When you change how you feel about your future; when you discover your true Primary Aim, the how will always find its way to you just as strongly as you desire to find it.

The hard part is not necessarily 'the how', it's more likely to be 'the why'.

Time and time again I've seen clients enjoy immense breakthroughs when they identify and build on their defined Primary Aim.

Primary Aims don't always have to be deep and meaningful either, and it might be that the one you choose when you're 25 is different again to the one you're aiming for at 50.

The classic metaphor used by just about every coach is that you can't buy a ticket at a railway station unless you state your destination.

Without this information there is no way you'll be able to walk away with that piece of card. Now imagine all the people around you who are prime candidates for coaching, who are doing exactly the above in their mental railway stations. They're going nowhere fast. In fact they're so busy going fast without a destination they are completely oblivious to the fact that their life lacks purpose. The sad part is that one day they're going to 'wake up' but after too much sand has disappeared through the neck of their hour glass.

Candid Coaching Conversations

Candour originates from the Latin *candor* meaning brightness or whiteness and *ego candeo* means I shine.

Here are some synonyms:

Honesty, simplicity, sincerity, frankness, impartiality, fairness, outspokenness, truthfulness, straightforwardness, forthrightness, openness and directness.

Provided you have rapport and a good relationship with your client, creating a state of candour will be an enormous asset in any evolutionary journey together.

A principal reason why coaching from a third party is always better than being coached by one of your colleagues is that the level of candour is greater between two relative strangers who are in rapport.

Getting this candour established as early as possible in the coaching relationship will speed results considerably.

It will also ensure that those commitments your client makes are taken much more seriously. To get to a state of candour you would need to ask some really candid questions:

- As you know the coaching is confidential, and I would like your agreement that we are completely frank, open and honest with each other. How do you feel about this?
- On a scale of 1 to 10, how candid are you prepared to be in all our confidential discussions?
- If I'm prepared to speak my mind and say how something is, without holding back, would you be prepared to do the same?

Let's Always Venture to 'the Edge'

This is also known as exploring the lion's den and being more daring and challenging during coaching. If Guerrilla Coaching was represented by the human body I am now talking about the heart.

You will immediately appreciate the intuitive quality of the heart as well as a feeling in the gut.

I know when I've been coached I always remember and appreciate a coach who has stretched me. A bit like doing a parachute jump, challenging me to stand at the edge of the aircraft door and look down despite the potential fear and trepidation that I am experiencing.

If you're not prepared to do more of this with clients, the guerrilla style may still be an acquired taste, but one I hope you will savour soon.

I also raise my hands and tell you of the various times I've occasionally triggered quite emotional responses in people and I've had to abandon a session and agree to pick things up at another time.

What I will not do and can never contemplate as a guerrilla coach, is simply carrying out my client's instructions where I am paid to hold back my inner feelings and instincts because it would be 'politically correct' or 'professional' to do so.

A good way to deal with 'the edge' is to make a quick mention about it at the beginning of the session so the person's subconscious has a hint of what's to come.

This is a scriptwriting tactic in horror films where the audience is being prepared for the final scene by having a glimpse of the ugly creature's hand early on.

A good edge-producing question is to ask: *"What should you be thinking of taking action on right now that you are hiding from or avoiding?"*

Question for you: Putting you on the spot again, I'd like you to give yourself a score out of 10 for how edgy your coaching is?

Scoring 10 would mean you're dangerous (in a positive way) and the score of 1 means you always like playing it a hundred percent safe.

Let's look at some of these scores and what they mean. If you scored 8, 9 or 10 then you are most certainly guerrilla coach material, and I can imagine you already attract quite successful people to coach who want to make a further leap forward.

If you scored 5, 6 or 7 I imagine you're a coach who has his or her moments where you stretch clients yet fear going too far in case you upset the client and maybe lose them. The solution here would be to go more to the edge when coaching without going to the absolute edge so stretch yourself not the client to start with. Be a little more adventurous with some of your questions and suggested more ambitious client commitments.

If you scored 3 or 4 then there are two possibilities. Firstly it means you're new to coaching and need more confidence, which will come through experience, or the other possibility is you've been coaching for a long while and uncomfortable about heading in new uncharted waters.

Here some self-coaching might be the answer and if you would like to find 'the edge' in your coaching you may consider using some of the Mind Changer tools in Chapter 4.

Finally if you scored 1, or 2 the really good news is you're up to Chapter 9 so there must be something in guerrilla coaching that has taken your attention if you are still reading.

Perhaps you should reserve full judgement until you've completed the book, reflected on a number of the ideas and tried some of the concepts particularly with long standing clients.

I was once asked by a writer for help to get back into her career as a novelist. After a few sessions I realised that there was some candid conversations to be had and we got to the bottom of things when she explained that her fear was to write another novel that would turn out to be a big flop.

Her agent had already said that she was probably not best seller material and this unfortunate comment was playing on her mind. Taking her to 'the edge' was challenging her to get a certain amount of her new novel on paper by a cut-off date. When she came out with her various excuses again, I explained that I would not be prepared to continue if she wasn't determined to take this all important step in the direction that we both agreed was the right one. There were a few e-mails and voicemails after the session and before the deadline and I'm pleased to say she completed what she had agreed, albeit that she apparently stayed up many nights writing before the deadline.

This was the boost she needed to continue to do more on her novel and eventually complete it. Although this particular novel has not been a runaway bestseller, it sold more copies than her previous three put together and she is now working on a new story that she's convinced will take her to the top. She also feel really positive about her future that she could not sense before.

"Which means that?"

If there's no action that follows all the dialogue in coaching, it makes a mockery of the entire process. Giving a client too many things to do is also counterproductive and reaching a place which stretches them rather than demotivates them is naturally where one should aim for.

Using the three words *which means that* helps to translate words into actions. For example, the client says to you "I really need to complete the report this month." My response: "Which means that?"

And I will keep using these three words until we have an action worth noting as a final commitment.

Commitment is Absolute

Some years ago I was coaching a group of managers attached to a well-known building society and I had given them 50 minutes for lunch. During lunch there were some delays in service that I was aware of, yet no one had approached me from the group to ask for an extension in time.

Given I was part of this group commitment I curtailed my three-course lunch and got back into the meeting room with a minute to spare only to find one of the eighteen managers sitting in the room.

She looked up and smiled at me as if to say, "We're going to have to wait for the rest of them". My reaction was to explain that I was now ready *as per the group agreement* to restart the afternoon session on time which I duly did.

The lady looked a little horrified that I was now coaching her alone and about 8 minutes later the rest of the group started to file back into the room and take their seats.

At no point did I stop the coaching until everyone had returned after a further 16 minutes.

I then proceeded with a little rewind and enquired as to what had happened to our agreement of a 50-minute lunch break. Excuses and explanations came thick and fast, mainly about the hotel having a service problem in the middle of serving lunch. Of the entire group only six managers eventually appreciated and wholly supported my staunch position that a commitment had been made and given there was no discussion to amend or change it, why did the group think it was okay to to completely ignore it?

This was a three-day programme and all of this happened on day one. I decided to do my utmost to open the minds of these future potential high flyers to the idea of what commitment really meant. By day three the number of managers had grown from six to sixteen with a couple of cynics still holding out.

However most of them left the workshop in no doubt why holding to a promise will feed one's soul and ignoring or failing to deliver on your word depletes who you are on the inside. Over the year that followed I received several e-mails from the group where people had used the power of commitment with themselves and members of their team to great effect.

It would have been so easy to have been really soft with them and said nothing about their lateness, perhaps even agreeing with them that they had every reason to be back later than the 50 minutes that was universally agreed. However as a guerrilla coach if you're not prepared to adhere to fundamental values at all times then why would you expect your clients to ever do the same?

Dare you consider Zero Tolerance?

Which bring us to some interesting questions:

- "Would you consider coaching with a zero tolerance policy where goals that are feasible in theory and practice must be adhered to?"
- "Would you absolutely hold your clients to this total no-nonsense expectation?"
- "Could you go this far and stick to your guns?"

This means taking them to task if they fail to deliver on their promises and it can be quite a lot to ask, particularly when many of your clients may also be dealing with your invoices.

When coaching I'm fair with clients yet never ever offer them an easy ride to carry favour.

Letting people off commitments because it is too embarrassing to challenge instead is *cowardly coaching*.

When the client fails, then the coach has also failed and naturally this is not a good sensory experience.

On the selfish side, the coach is also risking their professional reputation. There will be situations with clients that are understandable and allowable, but in reality they rarely occur. A question I have posed to coaches who are not keeping commitments is: *"If results aren't that important, why do you need a coach?"*

Coaching the Coach

Recently I sat with a fellow coach who had set up his own coaching business ten months ago. He was really doing well with a steady stream of new clients and he requested that I sit in a client session in order to offer my assessment of how he was doing and perhaps some pointers of how he could improve.

Given that he had set out initially to obtain a recognised coaching qualification, I appreciated that he was coaching very much 'by the book' and 'good luck to him' I thought.

His very first session was with a 41-year-old businessman and after some preliminary discussions he went straight into doing a personality profile. It was conducted rather like an examination where the client sat at a table and duly filled in the various boxes from an A4 sheet placed in front of him. After some initial deliberations around the results of the profile, he then went on to discuss goals and objectives. Once more this was done around the table and eventually he did suggest that the client take a more comfortable armchair. I need to add that the coaching was being conducted at the coach's home in the living room.

The session concluded with an understanding of what the client was looking for in the further five sessions on offer and after just two hours the client left with some handwritten notes.

Robert the coach, then offered to make me a mug of coffee and we sat down to review the session. I quickly put him at his ease and explained that overall there was absolutely nothing out of place with his professionalism and the method of dealing with his new client. Indeed, the client did appear satisfied that he had started something that he had never done before. At the same time Robert could see that I was holding back and intuitively asked me to put my cards on the table. Great, it was candid conversation time and I dived in.

"Fire in your belly." (Sensory)

Robert didn't quite know what I meant.

"Explain."

"I didn't sense any fire in your coaching, Robert."

We talked this through and eventually he had to agree that if he was to step back for a moment and think about the overall effect that the session had on his new client, the word 'satisfaction' sprung to mind, but 'fire' didn't.

He also agreed that there was no excitement in the process and as much as the client left with a smile on his face he certainly wasn't oozing with new enthusiasm or unbridled inspiration.

Left Brain versus Right Brain

Coaching, like any profession, have those who lean towards left-brain thinking which includes analysis, sequencing, order, organisation and things making sense versus right-brain thinking which includes creativity, spontaneity, intuition, instinct and gut feeling.

There's no right or wrong whether you coach to the left or the right, and guerrilla coaching isn't about being entirely right-brain about everything to the total exclusion of a more analytical and considered way of working.

So balance is perhaps the order of the day, and where Robert could have improved was to have been a little more effusive, energetic in his approach and certainly harder-nosed when discussing the client's goals and objectives.

The other thing that was missing was 'the edge'. There was nothing edgy in the two-hour experience for the client and as a result by not taking the client there, particularly this being the first session, Robert may have inadvertently set a softer pace for all the other sessions where the client was thinking low rather than high in terms of intended results and expectations.

Robert then asked the inevitable question: "If you were coaching the client using guerrilla tactics what would have been different?"

This was a great question yet it was important for me to assure him one last time that my answer was in no way a criticism of his performance merely a different option.

Coaching Session Rewind – using The Guerrilla Wheel

NOTE: I have used the wheel in subject order of importance

1: SPEED

This session was in two parts, the personality profiling and the actual coaching. I would have ensured that the profiling exercise was not officially part of the session in order that the experience would feel much faster overall.

Ideally the profiling should have been done online so the results would be ready at the start of the session. This first session should have been no more than 45 minutes.

5: LOCATION

Since it was a fine summer's day, I would have suggested the session should take place outside on the wooden decked area with a sun shade, a portable flip chart and laptop for any visuals required.

7: SENSORY

I would have requested that the client remove his jacket and tie to feel more relaxed and I would have followed suit. I would also have wanted intuition and gut feelings/responses to play a larger role in the session for both coach and coachee given it was the first session.

2: INTERVENTIONS

The three interventions I would have chosen for this first session would have been: *Mindset, Strategy and Self-Discovery*. It would have been good to ask some specific questions to get a feel for how serious the client was in embarking upon the coaching process. We would touch on Primary Aim, while also covering candid conversations, together with an understanding of 'the edge' and commitments.

So there would have been a poignant front end to this first session to make absolutely sure that both client and coach were in complete alignment. Why were we working together? What would the coaching consists of? How would the coaching work? And covering any 'what if' questions.

Connecting with the client would also be high on the agenda to ensure he was serious about achieving his desired outcomes. Until there was a strong client/coach 'agreement' in place there would be no point going any further.

6: EXPERIENTIAL

Getting the client on to his feet and start selling his goals and objectives to me would be an important step to ensure the client was really buying into what we were there to jointly achieve.

What could he tell me that would make me feel excited and passionate about working with him? Could he properly articulate his dream objectives? How would this make him feel?

3: MASTER PLAN

By the end of 45 minutes there should be an outline of a Master Plan in place with some basic agreed commitments to go forward.

In a worst case scenario if 45 minutes was just too short a time for Robert, who was new to coaching, one alternative would be to conduct two 45 minute sessions with a 15 minute break in between. But do always consider smaller 'islands' of time rather than large 'land masses'. Getting used to 45 minute sessions is also just a habit.

4: IMPLEMENTATION

A better discussion of how all this was going to work, what were his commitments and how he would be supported on this journey of discovery and ultimate achievement.

7: SENSORY

Throughout the use of *The Guerrilla Wheel* one of my personal coaching objectives would be to stimulate, excite and inspire the client so he'd feel a real a fire in his belly. Incidentally, I would also need to genuinely feel this sensation myself in order to ensure I pass it on to him.

Finally, to enhance the experience both from the experiential and sensory, I would have considered covering some Immediate Outcomes and/or deploy a Guided Visual.

Robert's Reaction

As a professional coach, he was completely open-minded to suggestions and possibilities for the future. The biggest shift for him was to realise that coaching can and should be much more dynamic and multi-dimensional; using something like *The Guerrilla Wheel* rather than creating an extension of a business meeting that would inevitably come across as more two dimensional.

The other insight for Robert was that he himself didn't get particularly excited, and if this was the case he appreciated that he couldn't expect his client to be any different.

As ever, Guerrilla Coaching doesn't have to be replicated in exactly the way I'm advocating. Most coaches may however consider taking certain levers and tools that they would find of value to enhance their own methods and approach.

Troubleshooting Guide

Here are the 12 challenges that coaches may encounter that we originally touched upon at the beginning of the book and suggested solutions for your consideration.

The Sensory element runs through most of them as you will see.

No. 1: There's no connection with the client

This should normally be a very rare occurrence unless the client is not hiring you as a coach directly. If a company or other individual has sent the coachee to work with you then this scenario may happen.

When I've had to deal with this situation, I've normally offered a little latitude by asking a few simple questions. Once I'm clear there is strong resistance, I would do a 'trial rejection' on the client. This would be something like:

> *"Just to let you know I would really love to work with you and right now I am seriously considering suggesting you work with another coach. Now please don't take this personally (they will of course) but I like to think that I've been very helpful to numerous people in your organisation already, and the evaluation that's come back on me has always been extremely positive. And in order to help you we need a solid working relationship (PAUSE AND MAKE EYE CONTACT). Would you like to discuss this possibility or should we call it a day?" (SILENCE UNTIL THEY SPEAK).*

This approach has worked well for me and yet there was one occasion when the person decided that she still didn't want to take the coaching any further. You can't forcefully coach someone and on the odd occasion it might be just as well to walk away at the outset. Hence the Sensory element is a key tumbler.

No. 2: No buy-in for the coaching

My first thought here is – who is paying for the coaching? It can't be the client if there is no buy-in. Unless this is the first (and last) session.

Buy-in is probably the most overlooked requirement in coaching. It starts with the coach getting a 'sense' of the person, evaluating how the client responds, observing their body language, listening to their tonality and ensuring there is some chemistry in evidence. Where there is a brick wall, some candour would be recommended. Naturally, as coach you should remain positive at all times. Finally, consider that the person may simply be having a bad day and recommend the session is reconvened.

Also check:

- Do they know your background and experience?
- Have you asked the 'why?' question sufficiently?
- Did you ask *how serious* they were as a score out of 10?

What about doing a fast forward to get them to sense and experience potential results?

No. 3: You are not sure how best to help a client

When a coach asked me how best to deal with this, I did remind them that true coaching comes from co-achievement which is a shared process.

To work out how best to help a client requires a joint discussion rather than the onus on your shoulders. This can be achieved as:

1. Have you asked the client for their dream list?
2. Have they described what they truly want?
3. Do you know what their Primary Aim is?
4. Have you ascertained what would make the biggest difference to them immediately?

No. 4: You feel you lack specialist knowledge

Before any coaching session do a little bit of homework on the client's industry/business/background. It's like going on holiday and not speaking the language. If you've picked up a phrase book on the plane and memorised half a dozen likely things you may need to say, then just making that attempt will usually create rapport with the nationals of the country you're visiting.

The same principle works in coaching. With the Internet today you can print out a lot of background information that you can even pull out and refer to in the session. The other point is that learning from your client and being interested in their responses will go a long way anyway in cementing a client/coach partnership.

No. 5: You fail to impress the client in the first session

Did you thoroughly prepare? If you look at *The Guerrilla Wheel* you will see the seven tumblers that potentially open the combination of the client's safe, also known as their mind. How many tumblers did you use? Did you drive the session and make it interesting whilst also proactively listening to your client and learning from them?

Looking to taking responsibility yourself, it may be a good idea to contact your client over the phone and confess that you too were not happy with the way the session went. Be honest and open, admit to not hitting the mark and suggest a way forward.

No. 6: You've done a good job but the client doesn't want to continue

Think TV soap. How many regular viewers would Coronation Street or EastEnders get if each episode was a complete self-contained story? Who knows what the exact number would be, though I can be sure it would be far less than the current audience rating. This is because these shows use a cliffhanger at the end of every episode. What's happened here is that you come to the end of a session and neatly complete it so it feels like there's nothing more to look forward to.

If in fact there isn't anything else you can help your client with then the coaching should come to a natural conclusion. However, 80% of all the clients I've ever worked with have a long endless list of future requirements.

One hot tip is to never identify a particular number of coaching sessions at the beginning of a client contract. This is sheer madness. How would you know how many sessions it's going to take unless you are clairvoyant? Indeed, if you've earmarked six sessions who's to say you couldn't do it in two?

No. 7: The client is not improving or achieving their goals

My first reaction is to enquire whether they're keeping all their commitments? If they are keeping their commitments then I'd want to ask:

- "Am I using the right interventions and coaching levers?"
- "Has the client identified their *real* Primary Aim?"
- "Could the objectives be perceived to be too big and they actually need to be smaller, more psychologically manageable parcels?" (We all know this, yet often fail sufficiently to create this sensation in coaching.)
- "Could I come up with some Immediate Outcomes that could be achieved in the next few days as a challenge and motivator to the client?"

The sensation of winning, the feeling of success is an immensely strong motivator.

No. 8: The client feels better but there is no tangible evidence of achievement...

This normally occurs when your coaching has been far too 'right- brain'. In other words the client has been set on a path to achieve things like: feeling better or being less stressed. Whereas these may be viewed as wins they are fairly intangible. Good coaching, guerrilla or otherwise, is about a balance between tangible and intangible outcomes. Go more to the left now, set up some hard tangible goals and after vetting them, creating a step by step plan to 'get' them.

No. 9: The client is initially sceptical

Have you given the client a candid outline of who you are, what you do professionally and in broad general terms what you've been able to achieve with past clients?

Sometimes you have to sell yourself to the client before you roll your sleeves up and get started with the coaching. On one occasion when I was confronted by this challenge I actually called one of my best clients and asked if they wouldn't mind speaking to my potential new client on the spot. This worked exceptionally well and took just 6 minutes.

No. 10: Client takes things with a pinch of salt

As a coach you must take full responsibility here because you've not communicated adequately as to why you're both working together in the first place. Also what the process is all about and how it could really impact their career/business/life, if it were to work properly.

GLEN: *Give me a score from 1 to 10 of how well you're doing in your career/business right now.*

CLIENT: *6.*

GLEN: *If there was a way of making your score 9 or 10 in a very short space of time, what impact would this have on you?*

CLIENT: *(Smiling) Massive but how could that possibly happen?*

GLEN: *You're right, there's no way of knowing whether this is feasible or not and it could be fun to find out. I'm game. How serious are you?*

No.11: Client fails to keep agreed commitments

Challenging the client's results surely has to be the only way you can deal with this. Of course being positive at all times is key yet papering over the cracks of failure will only make it more difficult for the client to make headway in the future.

I will always consider giving the coachee one last chance. If this creeps up to two or three you've lost your respect and they are just not in the zone anymore. Start the way you mean to go on in session one, and throw down the gauntlet if they fail to take things seriously the first time. If they do it twice consider asking them to get their cheque book out.

No. 12: Client not returning calls/e-mails promptly

There is something going on here that needs your attention. The solution is probably an amalgamation of all the previous solutions.

At the earliest opportunity ask the client (when they eventually do come back) for a strategic review of the coaching which may be by telephone and have a candid coaching conversation. You may need to re-sell the *why, what and how*. Then have an exciting *'what-if'* to get the client back on track.

We all need to be more sensory aware in order to give the best to those we coach. It's the deployment of as many of our five senses as well as the utilisation of them too. We all pay a lot of money for our senses to be stimulated – in the cinema, at a concert, from our mobile devices, in buying a car, choosing an ideal holiday and so on. Senses matter to us a great deal, it's the route to our soul. Using the Sensory Tumbler, even just considering its potential in coaching a client will enhance what you do every time.

10

BUSINESS BRIEFCASE

In the last five to six years the number of coaches describing themselves as a business coach has escalated dramatically. More people who coach realise that since the process is about helping people's performance you may still leverage success whether applying it to someone's life or their business. To an extent this is true though not completely the case.

These days when I work in a business, particularly a larger multi-national, no one is under any illusion that I'm there to sit with the financial director, chew over the latest P & L and help with the strategy or share price.

My work is all about people performance ranging from the CEO, the Board, managers, team leaders, creating performance insights, strategies, sales models, leadership alignment and communication improvement. Yet with the smaller business and particularly the sole trader, they are more hungry and often very needy for business catalysts that will help them in a more instantaneous and tangible way. Hence the business briefcase... of coaching tools.

If you're a coach who would like to work more with small businesses I hope this chapter will be useful in identifying a handful of business performance catalysts that supplement your people performance ones.

Recently a colleague told me of a newly-qualified 'business coach' aged 23 who was hired through a coaching company to coach a 56-year-old CEO. Apparently when the youngman walked into the room the CEO looked very dismayed. He very soon made the point that he had been running a business for over 25 years and could not believe or understand how someone aged 23 who had never run a business in his life was here in his office about to coach him.

As you would expect, the young business coach explained how he didn't have to be in business or have a MBA in order to help, and the coaching process was about asking key questions that perhaps the CEO had not considered.

Even so the meeting was very short and the contract with the coaching company was not taken up. This is perhaps where the guerrilla approach is a much more robust proposition. To go into a business of any size and make it clear that it's the mode of coaching, style, approach and focus on tangible results that will make a biggest difference.

In addition to this, having a small number of powerful and relatively immediate business wins to offer the company can be impressive if presented well. Imagine how more tantalising and intriguing this would be.

In business coaching, asking sound business questions is a necessary requirement but there needs to be more in your arsenal if you want lots of recommendations and a long coaching contract.

One of the early books I read that helped me immensely in business coaching was the bestseller *The E-Myth* by Michael Gerber. If you haven't read it, do so as soon as you can. The other book for the small business and in particular the sole trader is: *The 4-Hour Work Week* by Timothy Ferriss.

In the case of Gerber's good read, there were a couple of concepts I immediately picked up which had a big impact on coaching businesses in general. Even twenty years after the publication of the book, I still find it hard to find many small businesses that have fully grasped these dynamite ideas.

Strategic versus Operational

Earlier I looked at the In/On Strategy and this is a Gerber principle based on an original idea from T J Watson, the man behind IBM.

Are you working in your business or on it?

Are you just doing the things that businesses do or are you thinking bigger picture in a strategic way that will help you get to winner's enclosure?

In order to be even more strategic, one of his great questions to any business owner is: *"What is the purpose of a business?"*

Whenever I've enquired this of a small business, here are the top three answers:

- To make a profit
- To sell things and give good customer service
- To make money and expand while employing people

Here are the top three business textbook responses:

1. A commercial or industrial enterprise to provide goods and services involving financial, commercial and industrial aspects.
2. A legally recognised organisation to provide goods and services or both to consumers in exchange for money.
3. A commercial activity engaged as a means of creating livelihood or profit.

When you initially hear Gerber's definition to this same question you may be forgiven for not initially getting it. As a business coach if you're able to convey his idea to your small business client you could possibly transform not just their business, but their entire life.

"The purpose of a business is to sell it." (Michael Gerber)

Think of it this way, when people want to sell their houses normally a month or two before putting it on the market they give it a makeover and often spend some money doing so.

Isn't it also true if you've been in this situation, when you've done your makeover you look at your 'new' house and perhaps feel a desire to now live in it?

If we were to rewind this concept and the person was to have the makeover notion from the moment they moved into their home, they would have lived in a property with very high quality standards and enjoyed the experience over many years rather than only enjoying their home for a few weeks before selling it.

When we apply this principle to a business it makes perfect sense. If you run a business from day one in a way that it becomes really appealing to all who visit it, the chances of someone offering you a large cheque to buy it instantly increase. Remember, you don't have to actually sell it, but by thinking that you've created something valuable to sell from day one, you would probably own a business that's organised, well-run, bears a terrific brand and makes a tidy profit.

The Tears of a Printer

In 1997 I went to see a potential client in London who was a sole trader running a printing business. After some initial exploration, I asked whether I could take him through a small procedure that would get him to understand a key principle that I would ideally want to work with him on.

I sat him in front of a mirror and took out from my briefcase a golf hat with a wide peak at the front. On the back of the hat it said the work 'in' in large white letters and on the front of it just above the peak the word 'on'. When I initially placed the hat on his head the peak was facing forward and he could see the word 'on' as I proceeded to explain to him that 'on' was another term for strategic and what that actually meant in real terms in running his business. Then I turned the hat around to make him look somewhat silly with the peak at the back and the word 'in' easily recognisable albeit a mirror image. I explained that 'in' was about being operational, just doing things, and he nodded instantly fully appreciating the difference in terms.

We went on to discuss how much 'in' time he had in the last business week versus 'on' time. This seemed to be a relatively easy question and he explained that he had had a number of important jobs which meant that he was fulfilling orders and just doing things operationally as opposed to looking more strategically at the development of his business. So it equated to 95% 'in' and about 5% 'on'.

Moving on to the purpose of a business as defined by Gerber, I asked him a really searing question: *"Right now today, how much is your business worth if you wanted to sell it?"*

He thought about this for what appeared to be an eternity and then told me that it would probably be a few thousand pounds that covered the machinery in his office. Then it dawned on him that he had been running his own printing business for over 20 years and all he had to show for it was some printing machinery. I could also see a tear forming in one of his eyes. He had the stark realisation that he all he had created was a job, not a business.

This is where true business coaching comes into its own because as we continued to discuss the state of play he asked me why his other advisers from banks, accountancy firms and business support organisations had never ever explained this to him before. No surprise that he now desperately wanted some coaching and did ask whether there was still enough time to turn things around. There was and he did.

Lessons for a Sandwich Shop

I was once coaching a couple that decided to set up their own business for the first time. They decided they were going to set up a sandwich bar in a well-known North Yorkshire town and soon called me with the good news that they'd found the ideal premises.

When we met for the first coaching session I ran through the purpose of a business and I noticed how it completely got their attention. Within moments they were thinking differently about how they were going to set up the sandwich bar and what they had to do in order to sell it. Their evolution in thinking centred around some perceptual positioning as they were now putting themselves in the shoes of a potential buyer. There were already two or three shops selling sandwiches in the locale yet why hadn't anyone rolled up with their chequebook to buy these businesses? The reason of course was that these businesses were too busy attempting to make a profit to think about building 'a product' that was so compelling as a money-making machine that any entrepreneur or business baron with the smallest modicum of insight would instantly see and buy that business.

In a very short space of time they'd created a completely different type of sandwich bar with a number of new sandwich options that were very innovative. For example, 'The Godfather' was a lean baguette with pastrami, mozzarella, olives, anchovies and finely sliced chillies. It packed a real punch as you would expect from an item with that name. Now imagine a whole selection of sandwiches and paninis each having their own special theme. The way the sandwich bar was set out was unlike standard shops. It felt good to be inside and the food smelled delicious. Queues built up in the street and the entire enterprise became successful in a very short time. In fact it took just eight months before they had their first offer to purchase the small money machine as a going concern. They made so much money from the transaction that they were able to go off and set up a much bigger enterprise whilst purchasing an investment property at the same time. The last I heard, they sold all their properties and business interests and have moved to Australia for an early retirement in the sun.

The 12 Instant Business Wins

Here then are 12 immediate business wins from about 55 that I can normally share with a business client. My advice would be to start collecting your own tools and tips as you work with businesses when coaching. You'll find that the simpler the idea the more effective it is, because it's easy to imlpement. I would love to go into greater detail about these business levers, but given this is an introductory notebook on guerrilla coaching, there should be sufficient to whet your appetite so you may dig deeper yourself..

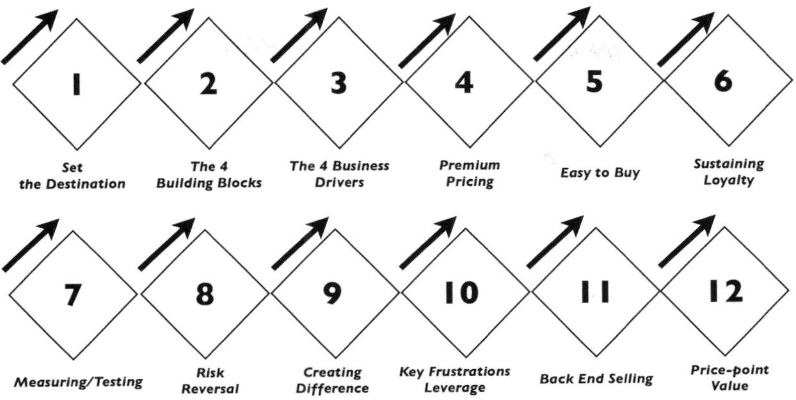

No. 1: Set the Destination

It sounds obvious yet few small businesses ever have this type of coaching. Here are some questions to ask:

- What was your initial reason for setting the business up?
- What is your current primary reason for trading?
- What are your short, medium and long-term plans for the business?
- Do you have any idea what your business is worth today?
- Do you have an exit strategy in place?
- What's your number one best selling product?
- Are you aware how your marketing strategy impacts sales?
- What is your dream outcome for you and the business?

Setting the destination is about ensuring they really do understand where they're going and most importantly why they're doing it in the first place. You could also link this to the Primary Aim of the individual/s running the business.

No.2: The Four Building Blocks

The four main things a business needs to think about for growth:

1. Increase the number of customers
2. Increase customer transaction frequency
3. Increase sales value
4. Create effective systems to run the business efficiently

To help a business create new customers and to get them come back will probably require some *Extraordinary Customer Care*. In my book of the same title, I do make the point that any business that delivers ordinary customer service will never win business from those that deliver extraordinary customer care as standard.

No. 3: Premium Pricing

Every business should have a premium-priced product. This is one with all the bells and whistles offering the very best for the truly discerning customer. In my case, my premium-priced product is Guerrilla Shadow Coaching.

It's premium-priced because of the amount of time involved and the intensity of the coaching required. It's certainly something that I wouldn't do very often, but the product exists, it is available and the fee is considerable.

The very fact that you have a premium product will say much more about you and the business. Furthermore, how can you sell something that no one knows about? I always ensure the business takes their premium product and gets it good exposure in their brochures or on their website. In normal business practice to create a premium product rarely requires any funding. It's what many would refer to as a 'no- brainer'. If the business has a premium priced product or range, what's the downside? And then consider the upside.

No.4: Make it Easy for the Customer to Buy

I went into a quality retail store to buy various items of clothes, came up to the cash desk and placed them on the counter. The manager looked at the number of items and was probably seeing a boost to the day's sales target. Yet when it came to pay she told me I had to use an alternative card because they didn't take this one. I was staggered. This store is being picky about taking a customer's money. In fact I was so underwhelmed that I left the clothes on the counter, bid her a good morning and left.

What the store was trying to gain in not taking a partcular charge card they had also lost in sales that would have been much more profitable. There are too many businesses that make it difficult or too complicated to buy and telling a customer to take their money elsewhere is sheer madness.

A long time back when I went through a period of addressing sales teams to encourage them to buy a place on my sales workshops, I found it relatively easy to get most of the audience to a point at which they absolutely wanted to attend, yet I made the buying process far too complex. It consisted of asking them to give me their business card at the end of the session, then my secretary would ring them to organise the sending of a cheque or the taking of credit card information. But people *buy on a high and say no on a low*. When these potential customers were contacted they were no longer on a high and buying a place at my seminar was suddenly a low priority. I therefore had to make it easier to buy. What I ended up doing through consultation with my bank, was to create a really simple form that required the customers name, address, name of their bank and the approximate location of the bank. That was all apart from their signature. I didn't need their sort code nor their account number and with this form I was able to send it to their bank and get a cheque back in return. It was brilliant and my sales soared overnight. I simply made it easier for my customers to buy.

Then you have web designers who make it painful when you decide to buy the product being advertised. It's sometimes not clear how you buy the product and you have to search various pages until you finally find out how to make the purchase. I wonder how many customers they lose who just can't be bothered. When coaching your business client, check out how easy it is to buy from them and do an assessment. It's normally 'gold dust' information.

No. 5: Sustaining Loyalty

This business win is giving customers a reason to come back to you. Starbucks offer a Starbucks card which gives you access to w-ifi in their locations as well as no charge for creams and syrups in drinks. They will also create offers for Starbucks cardholders from time to time. Café Nero and Coffee Republic offer a small loyalty card which gets stamped for every coffee you purchase and once it's full you get the next coffee for free. Then there's Nectar, travel points for airline travellers and so on. It would be a great coaching session to work out some new way of rewarding and bringing back the customers of a particular business as a self contained guerrilla session.

No.6: Measuring and Testing

Some business guru like Peter Drucker once said that what you can measure you can manage. In business marketing, there's a great little concept called something called 'split run testing'. The idea is to put out two adverts out that are exactly the same into different locations to see which one picks up the most business. This can be taken a stage further where two adverts are placed in the same publication though one advert is worded differently to the other, and again a comparison is made to see which one pulls in most interest. Getting a business to test their advertising and marketing and measure results is really worthwhile, and you'll appreciate it's the smaller businesses that always need the nudge to try this.

No. 7: Risk Reversal

Risk Reversal sounds a liability though in reality it isn't. The simple premise is that you create a proposition where you appear to take all of the risk and the customer takes none at all. A case in point was the wedding photographer who noticed that he had about six competitors within a two-mile radius and in the Yellow Pages his advert was just one of many that said more or less the same thing. How could a customer really differentiate? So he decided to change his advert and unlike the competition it said the following:

Your wedding is probably one of the most important events in your life. The worst thing imaginable is something going wrong with the photographs or video as these items are normally irreplaceable. When you use our services, should the worst happen we guarantee the following all at our expense:

- We will rebook the church
- We will rebook the reception and re-invite the guests
- We will rebook the cars
- We will pay for all the food and beverages
- We will re-photograph and/or film the entire event to your total satisfaction. *We are absolutely serious about getting it right for your special day!*

This is some guarantee! Yet think about the chances of the photography going wrong if they are careful and double check everything they take. Now they truly are differentiating.

There are many ways you can enter into a guarantee or reverse the risk for a client and I say to clients: *if it scares you, then maybe you need to check your products/services out because they may not be up to scratch.*

Once more this is a great offering to a business of any size and the coaching that goes with it should be as creative as possible. When guaranteeing a service it's suggested that the guarantee is about repeating the service for free as opposed to refunding money. Retail giants Tesco came unstuck when their *double the difference price guarantee* was abused by a small number of determined customers who lacked integrity.

No. 9: Creating Difference

On the same lines, here's a further angle on difference. We are all aware of what a USP or Unique Selling Point is. Businesses too use this term and talk about being different yet the reality is quite something else. In a coaching session you may wish to put the client on the spot and ask them to list all the things that they perceive to be different about their business and what is so unique about them. When I do this in a session just about everything a client lists I discount because I know competitors offer the same thing. For example, good service, wide choice, quick turnaround, great discounts etc. While we're on the subject you already know what my USP is – what's yours?

This is also an excellent question for your business client and the solution is important if they want to differentiate and be more profitable by winning more business.

If your coachee is stuck for an idea, you could get them to explore what differentiates Starbucks from other coffee shops in the marketplace, and at the same time do a similar exercise with Apple Computers.

Though every company will probably provide a long list of their differentiators, the one that applies to both Apple and Starbucks in my opinion, is definitely *extraordinary* customer service.

No. 9: Key Frustrations Leverage

This immediate business outcome comes from brainstorming the key frustrations that customers regularly face. When using this idea to help a business I've often suggested that I run a client advisory board session for half a day and meet customers to discover what their key frustrations are.

Once identified, the way forward would be to work with the business to iron them out and create solutions to overcome them. This is also a good question for a coach to ask their own clients along with thinking about how many of these tools here could be applied accordingly.

No. 10: Back-end Selling

Every time you go into a supermarket and are standing by the checkout there is some back-end selling going on as your eyes rove across sweets, mints and other additional purchase opportunities. In TV shopping there's back-end selling when you order your new piece of exercise equipment and they offer you the supplementary heart monitor or protection gloves once you've bought the initial product.

Remember too that people *buy on a high and say no on a low.* Smaller businesses are constantly forgetting the opportunity to back-end or cross-sell. You realise I'm sure how this one topic can provide enormous help to the bottom line of a business in a single coaching session.

When your client takes action and does something about it, they will end up getting the investment back that they made in your coaching many times over.

No. 11: Price-Point Value

When you give a reason and explain why you are charging a particular sum of money and really ensure that your prospective customer values your offering, there is normally very little resistance in proceeding with the purchase.

Let's imagine your dishwasher isn't working and you have two numbers to call. The first company you ring up and you explain the situation and they say it will cost £68. You thank them and say you'll let them know. Then you dial the second number and when you ask for a price from them they say £98. Just as you're about to say thank you but no thank you, the person who's quoting the price runs through *the reason* for the stated amount. She explains that a full diagnosis will be made, new parts will be used in the repair, that the engineer will arrive in an agreed half-hour time frame. Furthermore that the engineer will have full identification and will leave your kitchen exactly as it was found with any mess from the repair being cleared away. Finally a 90-day no quibble guarantee.

Then you compare this conversation with the previous one that simply quoted £68 and saying that they couldn't tell you exactly when the engineer would be calling but hopefully sometime in the morning. Which one would you choose?

This same technique can and should be used in all types of selling.

In short, *People want the why when they buy.*

Business Coaching Checklist

Potential subjects a coach may wish to tackle from their business briefcase could also include:

- Brand and image
- Personal and team success
- Business success and exit strategies
- Presentation skills

- Effective business communication
- More business customers/greater market share
- Extraordinary customer care
- Sales models and more effective selling
- Culture shift and evolution
- Leadership greatness
- Coaching
- Creativity
- Success planning

Classic Reasons why Businesses Succeed – for client discussion

- Strong Forward Vision
- Mission and Purpose identified by all
- Less dependence on specific individuals
- Great simple systems
- Excellent Marketing Strategy
- Business goals communicated regularly to all
- Insightful knowledge of the competition
- Performance standards that everyone signs up to
- Extraordinary Customer Service
- Inspirational and motivational leadership
- Excellent communication processes
- Fun as part of the Business Journey

Subjects that Small Businesses often need help with

- Financial record keeping
- Financial control
- Focus and vision
- Business plans and planning
- Brand and image
- Marketing
- Sales
- Debtors and creditors
- Customer care systems
- Leadership and management

If you've not yet ventured into coaching businesses, you may wish to consider starting with a sole trader or very small firm. Like most things, the more you do it the more confident you'll get and if you want to grow your own coaching business then working in the business sector is a must.

FINAL THOUGHTS

I've always believed that it's a great privilege for anyone to want to work with you. As a coach this is most certainly the case. When you end up helping to create an evolution, transformation of results or change of fortunes for the client the intangible reward can be immense and extremely gratifying.

For me it has to be about measurable results and therefore Guerrilla Coaching is not about tick box exercises in performance management. It's also a more radical and unashamedly non-traditional approach to making a difference and making things happen. If I thought doing handstands would double the ROI for my client then I would have also written a book called *Handstand Coaching*.

I have now re-read my ten chapters and want to sit down and re-write all of them. If we lived forever I probably would, but as we don't and time is ever looking over one's shoulder I must allow this version to go to my publisher.

Here's hoping you've got at least a handful of useful ideas that you can use, one new tool or concept that will take you forward in your own coaching adventures.

If you are just starting out, I am excited for you. A whole new world of possibilities awaits. Enjoy!

And so what would my parting suggestion be?

Well you should explore *The Secret* by Rhonda Byrne on DVD or in book form if you haven't already, then go on to see *The Karate Kid, Dead Poet's Society* and *The Shawshank Redemption* in that order. If you've seen all of them before, then see them again with new *guerrilla coaching awareness*.

And if you've been coaching awhile, I thank you for having the open-mindedness to bear with me and read what may have come across as obvious, well known to you or slightly 'off the wall'.

I hope you can tell I am passionate about my subject and would dearly like to make this book one of my genuine contributions to a profession that has sustained me while also sustaining the lives, careers and dreams of others.

May I sincerely wish you every future success...

Glen McCoy

INDEX